I0484680

THOUGHTS ON SCIENCE, RELIGION AND LIFE

THE MUSINGS OF A SCIENTIST

Thoughts: Eupsychia

Photography: Azad Harripaul & Eupsychia

ISBN:1461031419

Eupsychia

ISBN-13:9781461031413

DEDICATION

To those who question and think
and
are in awe and wonder about the world around us

Thoughts on Science, Religion and Life: Musings of a scientist

I think, therefore I am

I am scientist with a PhD– that is the most you will ever know of my identity - because any other information is going to categorize and stereotype me and any ideas will then be taken within the context of factors reasonably beyond my control – my gender, my religion, my nationality, my place of birth, my sexual preference, my race, my political ideologies, my physical attributes, how I dress, and the name I carry. You will ask me where my last name comes from to be able to understand my origin and my family lineage. You will stereotype me and categorize me and have your expectations of me borne of brainwashing – of what I should do and not do, think and not think, believe and not believe.

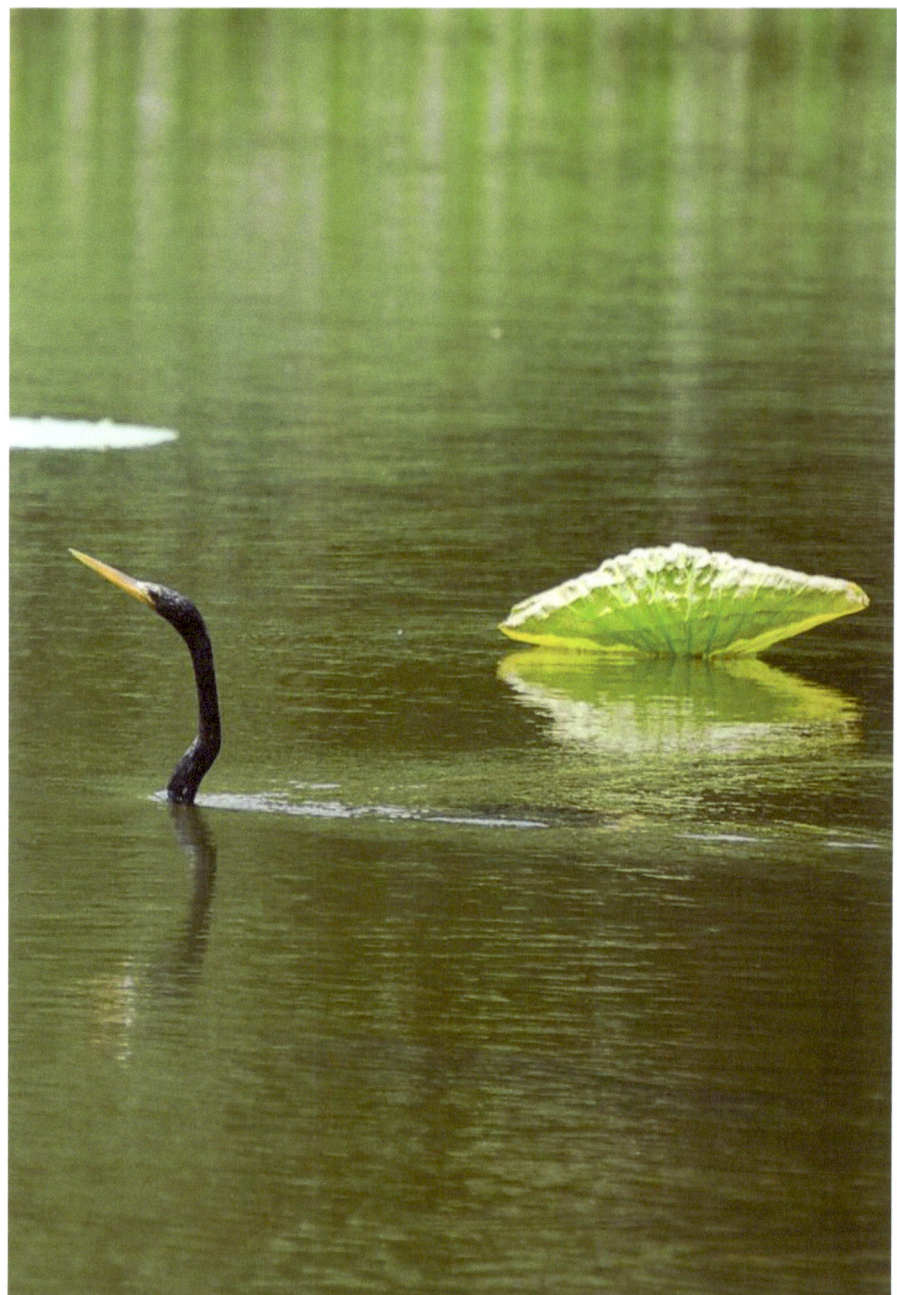

It is not your fault...it is nature's efficient way of processing information. And you would already have biases for and against, to some of those factors and preconceived ideas of whom I should be and what I should therefore believe and what groups I should identify with. You will hardly be neutral to me. You will argue with me to the ends of time of belief systems as though they were empirical systems once you perceive I don't belong to your grouping. So why did I choose to reveal the 'scientist' aspect of my identity?

Experience has shown me, that of all the things I am, it is the most universally respected attribute about me. The world listens to scientists and for good reason too – they have a damn good track record. You owe the microwave, cell phone, television, internet, electricity and medical wonders primarily to scientists - not politicians, not historians, not artists, not writers nor dancers. As Max Born, German Physicist remarked "Scientists themselves are an inconspicuous minority, but the impressive successes of technology give them a decisive position in society'

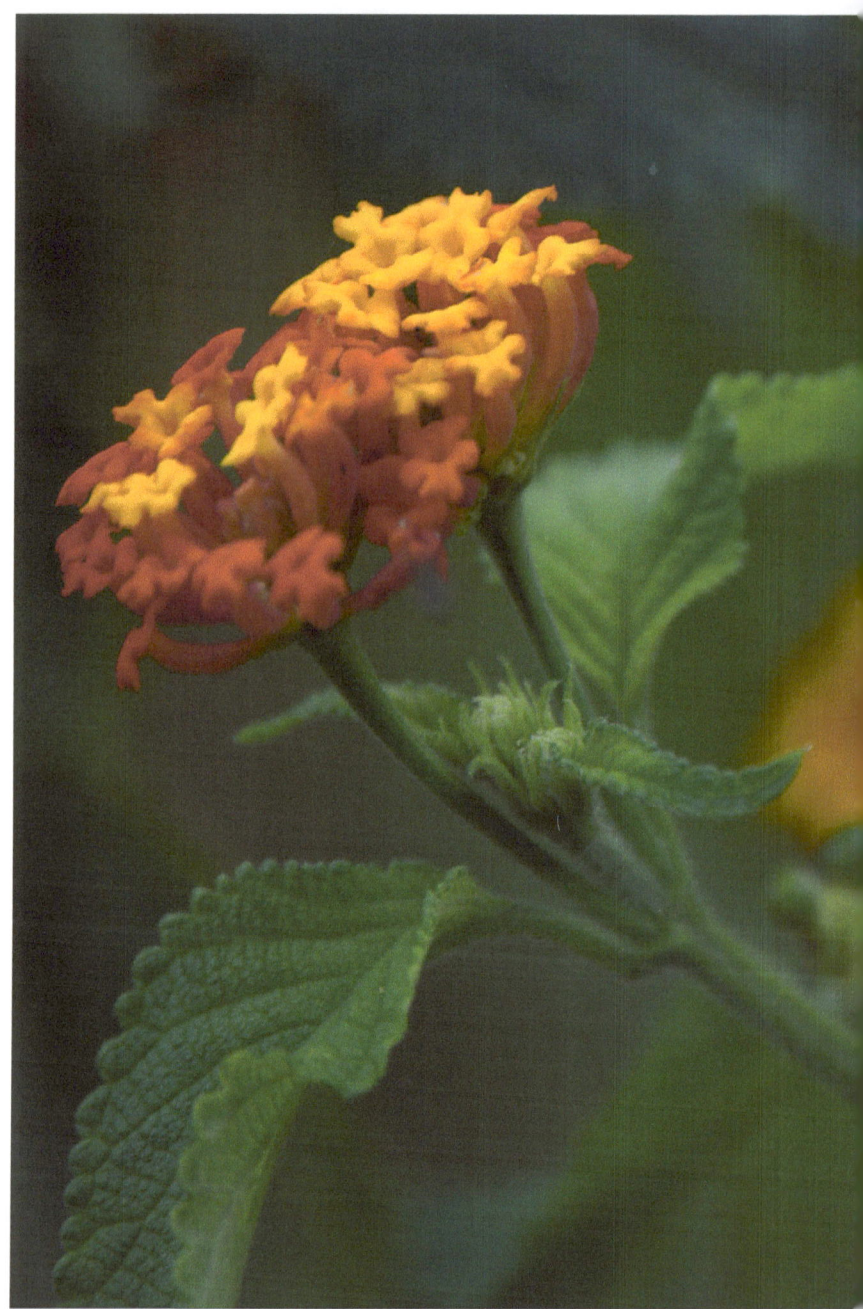

To have reached

We live in a fantastic time. Never before has humanity made scientific progress as in the present times – we have seen further out into space and deeper into the atom than we could have dreamed of a couple of hundred years ago – a staggering scale of 10^{40} powers. We have flown higher, faster and further than ever before. We understand the human biological systems and seen unbelievable diversity of life forms in the depths of oceans and on land. We have seen more magic and untold beauty in the Universe than ever before.

The last century has seen the decoding of the atom, development of the computer and discovery of the DNA as the basic building and programming block of life – this has launched us into the technological revolution and now armed with computational expertise we are finally able to peer into the workings of the brain like never before. We stand at the brink of answering philosophical questions like "What is consciousness?" even as we have earnestly and very seriously begun to address how life arose and is sustained in this universe.

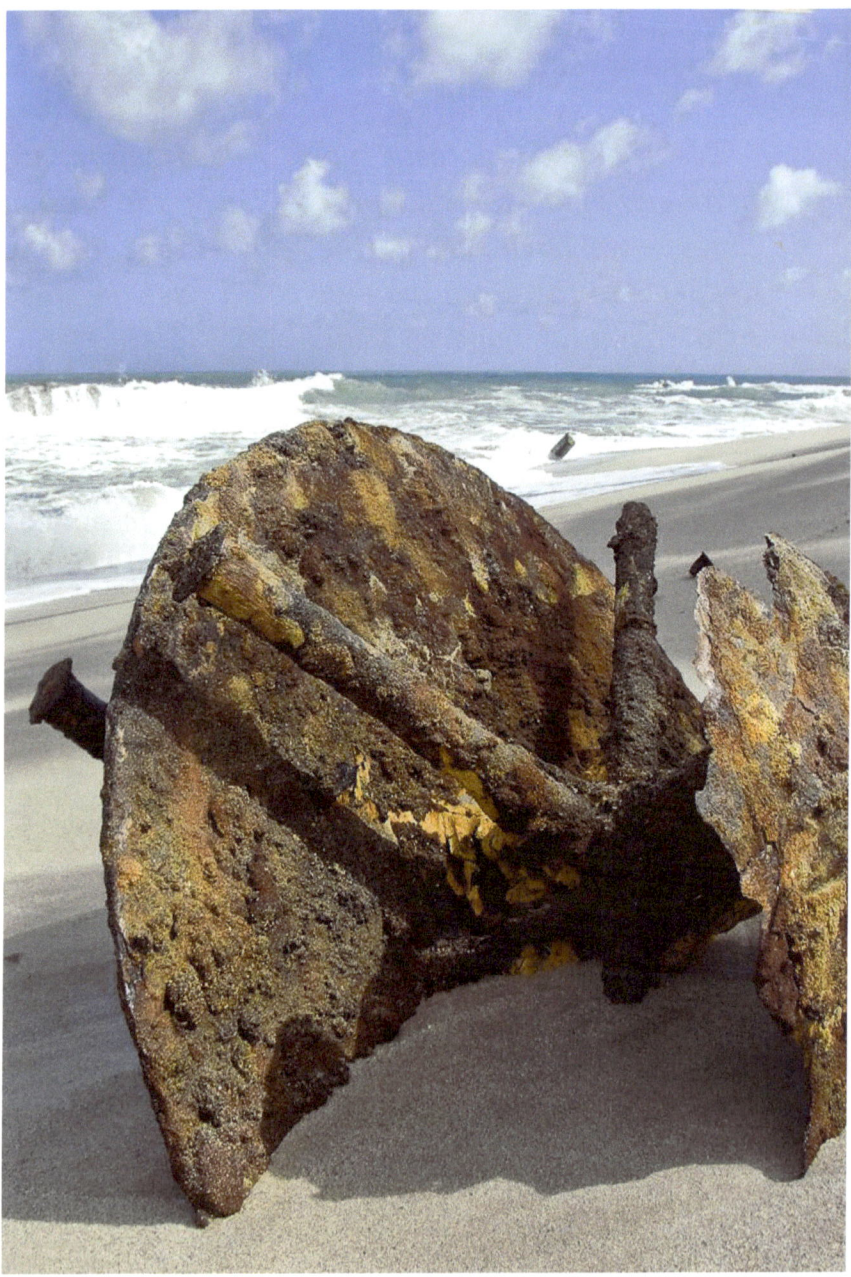

Pathway to heaven?

I have a few things I want to say. A few ideas that seem self-evident to me. If I was born in a Muslim home, I would be so grateful I got the final uncorrupted version of religion. If it was in a Christian home, thank God, Jesus died for my sins and I am saved for I would know the only path to heaven is through Jesus alone. If I was a Jew, I would know I was the chosen few. If I was born in a Hindu home – I would secretly thank my lucky stars that I don't have to deal with the concept of hell like Christians, Jews and Muslims and my life becomes philosophical about striving for perfection and in ways I become immortal through reincarnation. Each religion is nothing more than a code for living according to a set of rules in the final analysis.

So, if you are reading this – were you born into the religion you say you belong to or spent a significant portion of your life in? Chances are ninety five percent you practice or have practiced in the past, the religion you were born into. That speaks volumes for the notion that are we truly independent in our thoughts?

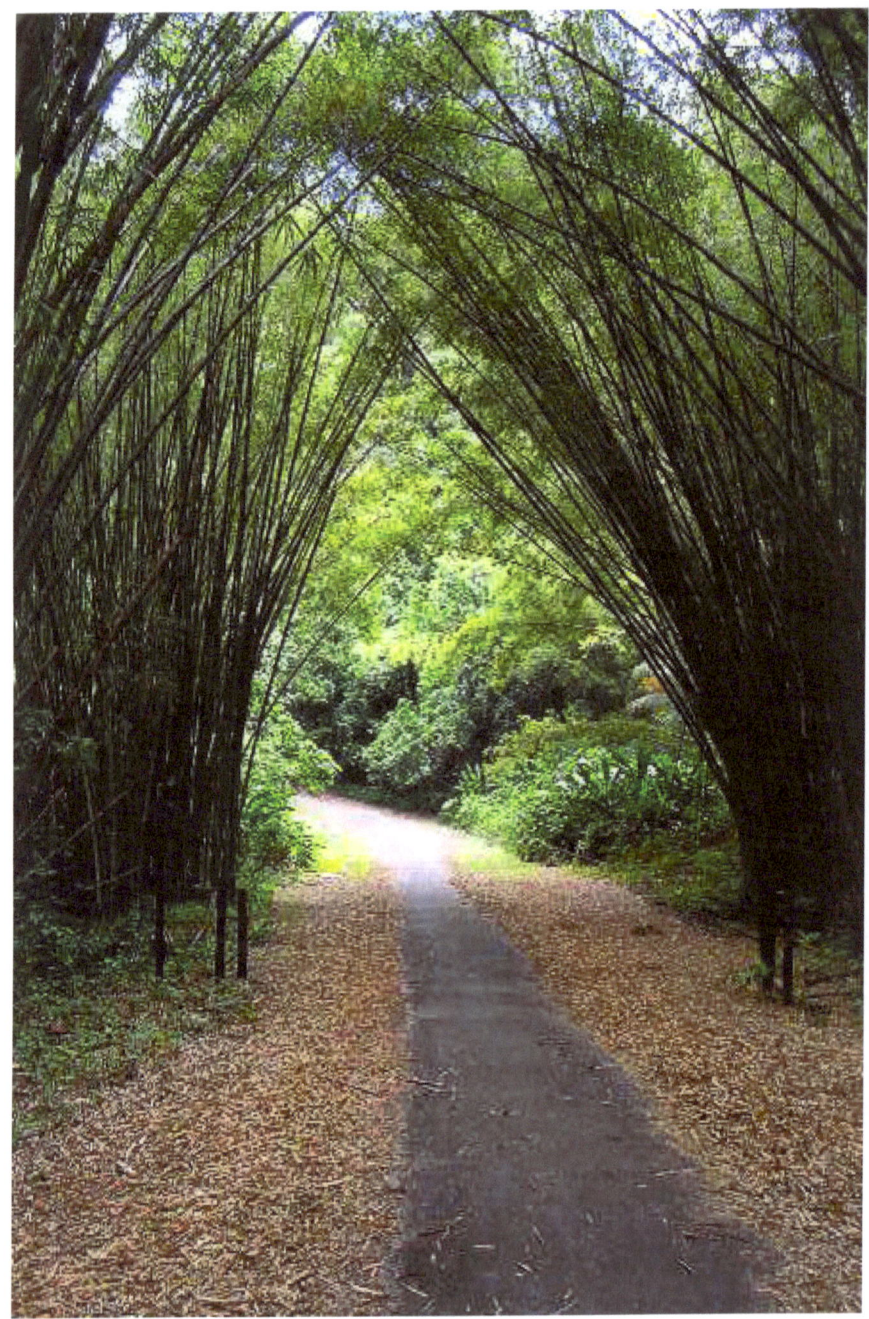

Each group believes they are right to the exclusion of the others. Nothing invites greater prejudice, arrogance, racism, than this foundation of all religions which is irreconcilable for time memorial. Watch the religious spread across the world map. Hinduism belongs to the Indian continent – Middle East is dominated by Muslims, Europe and Americas by Christianity. Could this be evidence that the religions that majority of us embrace is thrust upon us by brainwashing in our homes and environment? We have hardly chosen that which governs our daily lives and much of what we do and think.

Don't you get it? The distribution of religions is geographical in pattern more than a random data. Nearest-neighbour statistics would easily scientifically show up such patterns. Ever noticed that Hindu Gods are conceptualized after the animals on that Asian continent? There are no bears and seals, but monkeys, snakes, elephants, and cows. It is cultural and what people were familiar with and could identify with.

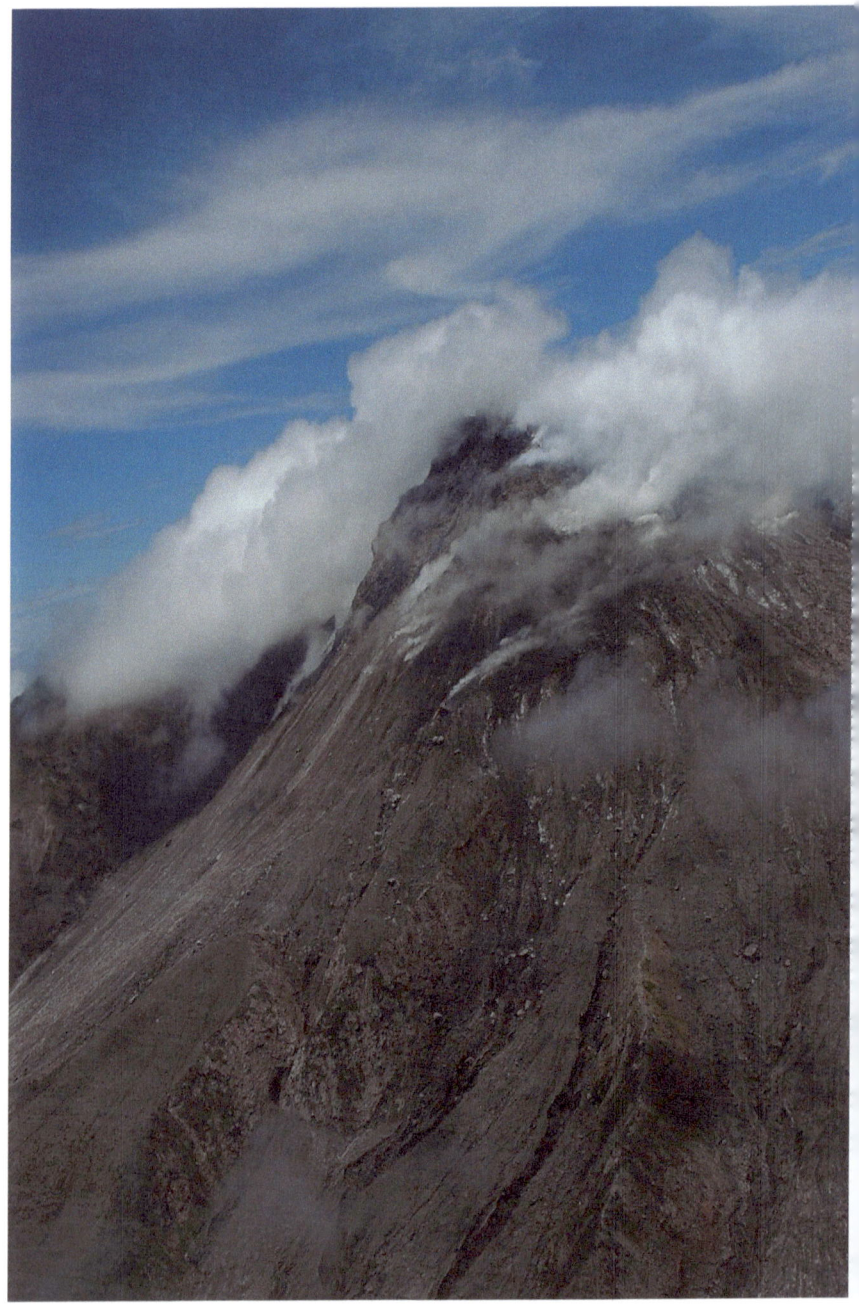

Question then becomes, did humans invent religion? That is a separate question from the existence of the creator. Are the details of religion nothing more than cultural conveniences?

Muslims fast without water – coincidental that they were desert people? Christians fast eating fish only for Lent. There were lots of fish in the Mediterranean sea. Hindus are vegetarian – and one should be if your Gods are conceptualized in animal forms. Are these mere coincidences or hinting at the cultural aspect of religion?

Religion is good. And it is supposed to embody all that is good. Than why and how do religious humans kill and torment and torture in the name of religion. It does not compute. It cannot compute. Why are women suppressed in all religions? When biologically they are similar to men and have the same needs, hopes and desires? Why women with intelligence and capability to add to the growth of humanity not given an opportunity for such in many religious societies ?

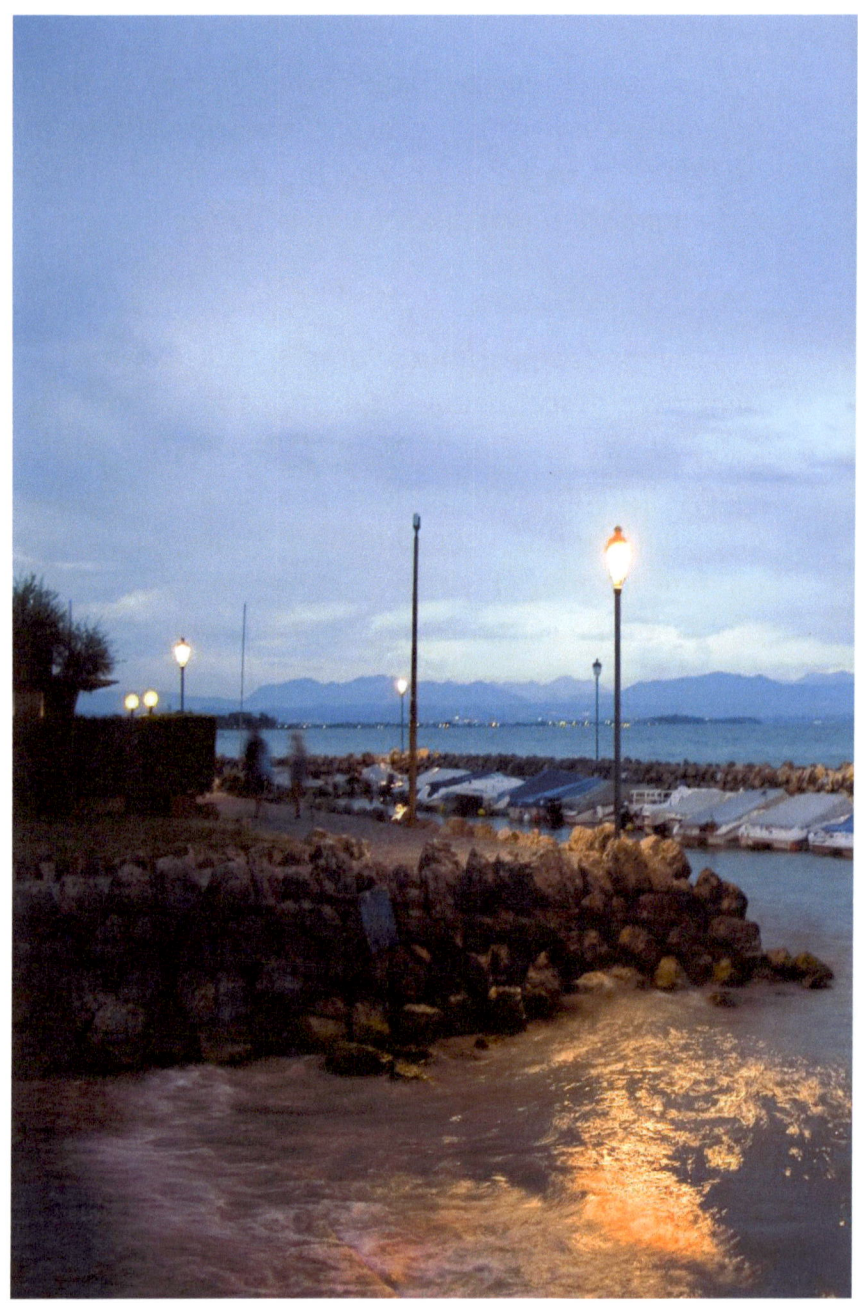

Who made these rules? Can the creator who created equal, lay down rules that are discriminatory? Or is it a ploy by one group to maintain power over the other?

The scientific method is treated like the Holy Grail – because science has been the most successful human enterprise in the last few centuries spurred on by the "scientific method" that encourages rigorous analysis, discussion and most importantly doubt. Religion does not encourage rigorous analysis, discussion and doubt and the tenets of a religion are not falsifiable like a good scientific theory.

This weakness is their strength and it is precisely for this reason that all religions survive. How can anyone out there prove to me, yes, prove to me without a shadow of a doubt that your religion is the correct and absolute thing? You cannot. And do you know why ? The answer lies in the fact that all religions exist today!

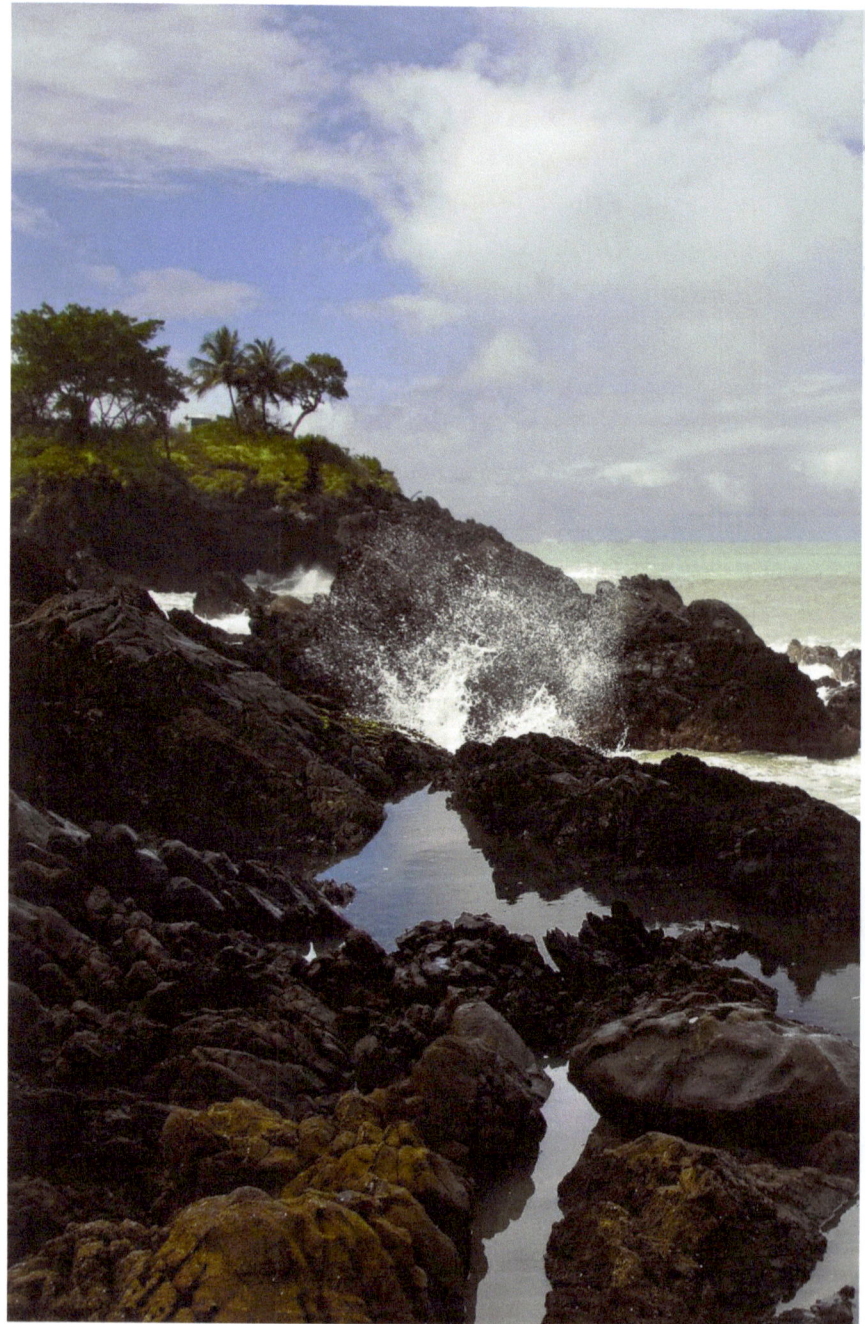

If we could prove beyond the shadow of a doubt which was the correct one, we would all be practicing it. If we could prove that God existed, we would all be believers. If we could prove that God did not exist, we would all be atheists. So no one really knows.

So why be hoggish and intolerant of another's belief systems recognizing that it is simply no more than that. The brainwashing they received in their upbringing and socializing roles. Why go around trying to convert people to your religion? Is there any greater arrogance than that and intolerance of that which you yourself practice?

The fact that we argue about anything, tells us that either side is not proven. When was the last time, you witnessed an argument of whether gravity causes things to fall to Earth or that a flame would heat a pot of water or that clouds produce rain?

Humans easily agree on thousands of provable things.

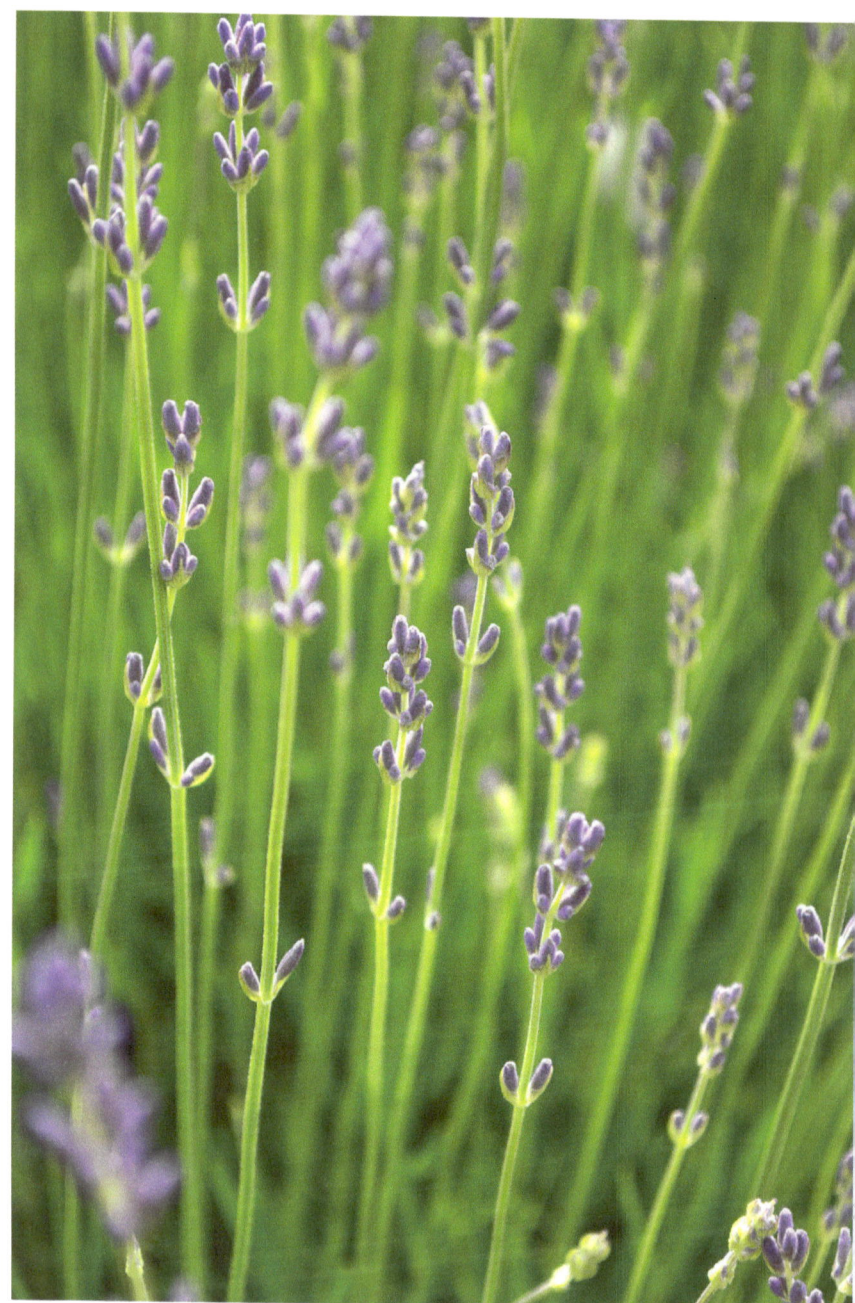

So, my point ? Why fight each other in the name of religion? Why judge someone of another religion? You are no better or more blessed than them. Do you know the greatest tragedy? There are things we likely will never know. And when we can, it will be too late for us. To know without a doubt if there is an afterlife, we need to die. It will be too late.

Religions nevertheless are wonderful things – in no other system lies the rules for good living as in all religions I daresay. Lying, stealing, murder and adultery are all frowned upon. It is a great recipe for good living – in all religions. Yet, every religion within its own self has its sub division that assumes it is better than the rest – Seven Day Adventists, Jehovah Witnesses, Roman Catholics, Sunnis, Shiites, Brahmins. How can every group be better than the rest simultaneously? It simply does not compute scientifically.

Religions preach no killings. Yet, it was a rare person like Gandhi with his ideology of nonviolence who actually practiced that. More wars have been fought in the name of religion in the history of mankind than anything else.

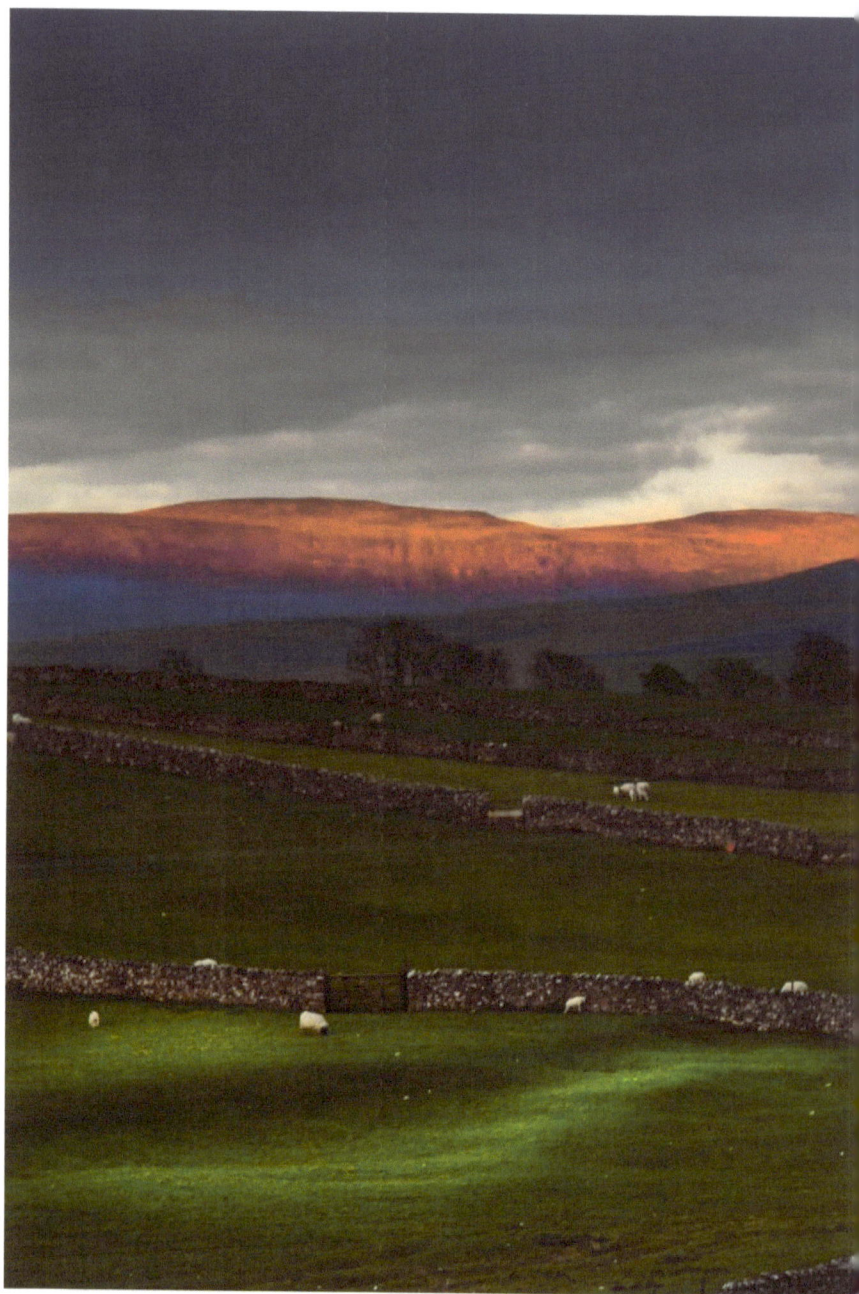

Turn the other cheek, Christianity says but they burn witches at the stake and crusades committed some of the worst atrocities. Forgiveness is nobler than revenge say Muslims – yet they blow up innocent victims.

How many have died in the name of religion between Israelis and Arabs over the Gaza strip? Is it really about God at all? Or simply about us - humans? You grow up in a war psychology and you know nothing else. You are brainwashed into it from childhood. Religion is culture. Culture is religion.

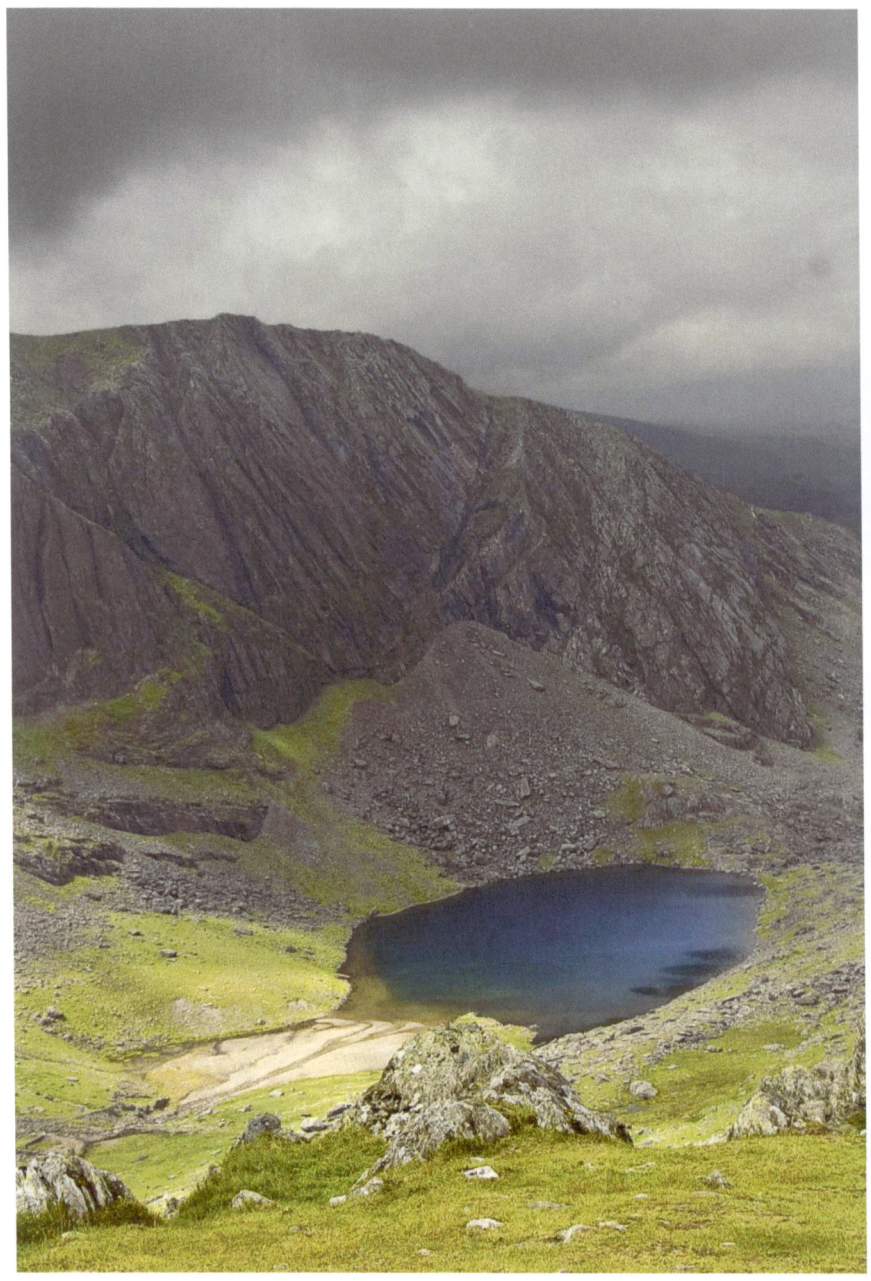

To touch heaven

Can't we respect diversity rather than trying to overwhelm and overcome anything that is different from us? Imagine every group thinking that it must reign supreme. We will simply kill each other out.

Striving for excellence in art, music, dance and sports...what role do they play in religion ? It is an aspect of us that makes us human and differentiates us from the rest of the animal kingdom. Can you make it to heaven for producing a great work of art or using your God given abilities to the limit? This is never preached in any religion.

Life is hard. Just getting through this life, could it not be enough to earn us a place in heaven? It is not easy being here. We found ourselves here. We have no choices. I am a scientist, I ride in an air conditioned car on the hot days and I see people selling in the torturous heat on the highways — working far harder than I do! But I am respected more, because I was blessed with brains, and opportunity? My only claim is that I worked to be where I am just like the man on the highway. Our efforts may be same, his perhaps more than mine and my rewards are greater. Do I really deserve it?

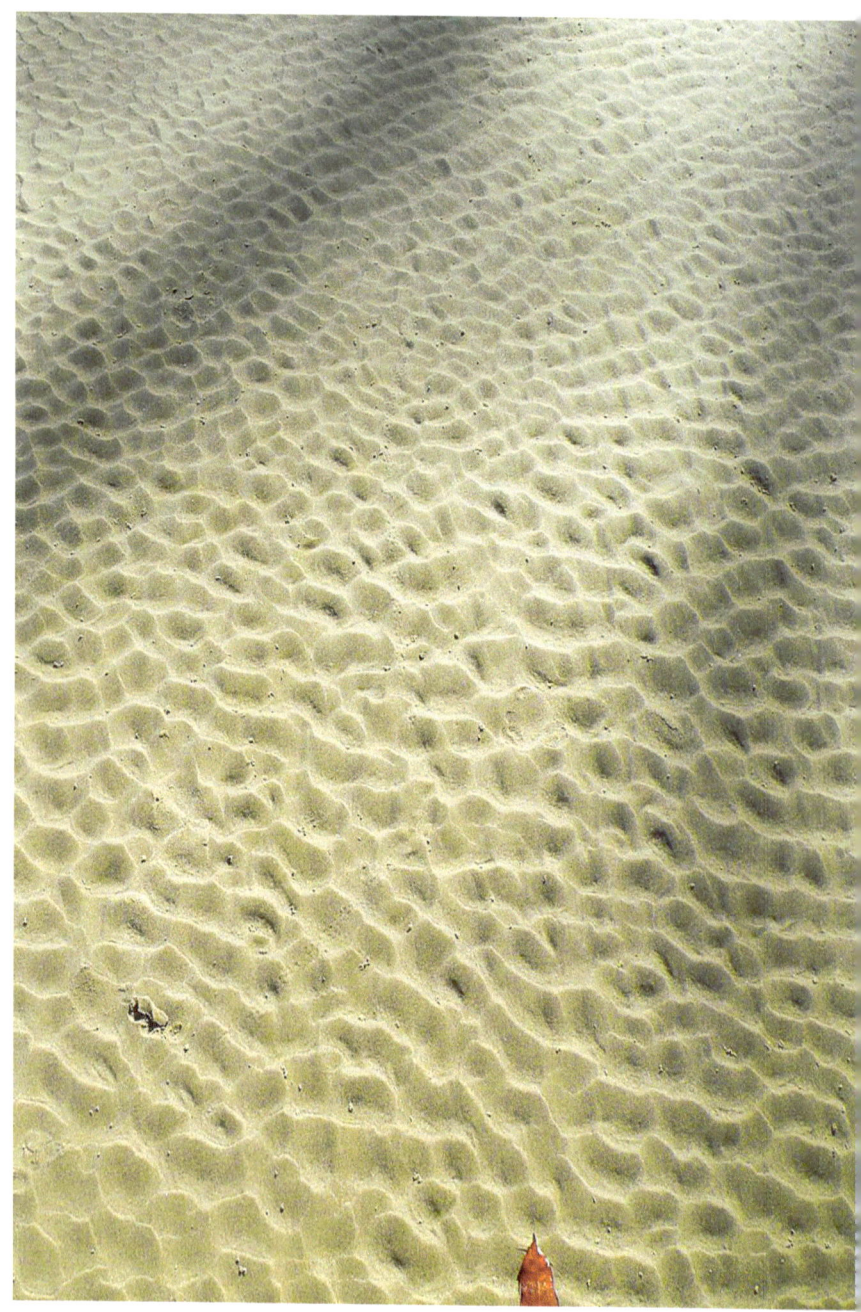

Could we not make it to heaven for effort so we stop judging each other for piety?

If you were blighted with a gene for drunkenness and had just a fraction of your life sober or had a bad temper and controlled it – should you not deserve to make it to heaven? Today we know that so much of who we are is coded in our genes.

If you did not hurt another too much , took care of yourself and left the world a better place than you found it, if you were not a burden to family and society, and you worked for an honest day's hard earned money, couldn't that get you to heaven ?

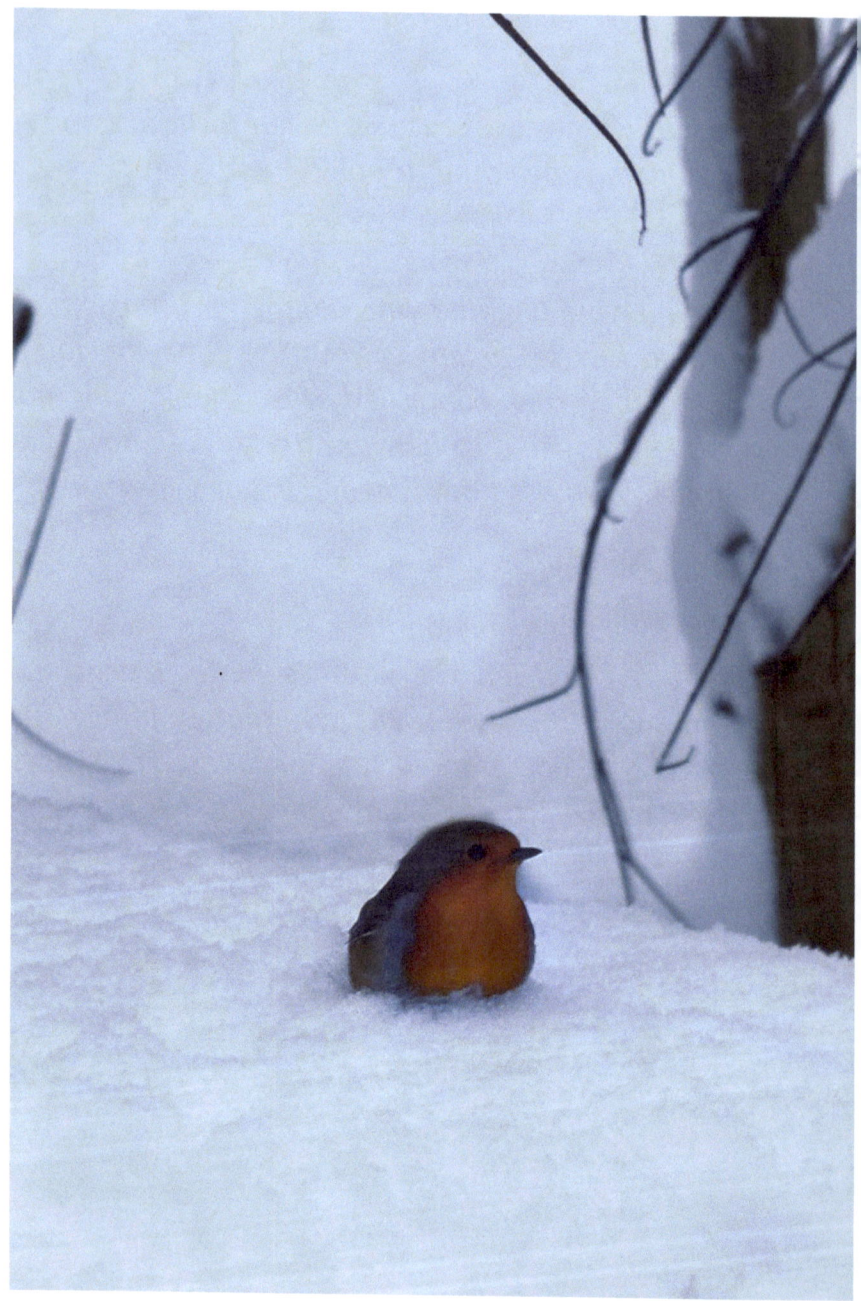

In heaven

There are those that walk among us endowed with a sense perception more sensitive and deeper than others. This is the realm of creativity. They sense things in a higher realm. Artists, writers, poets, musicians, and dancers have sense perceptions the rest of us do not and cannot understand. They see and create things we cannot. Science too in its final essence is art. How can anyone understand, how Albert Einstein had the intuitions that he did to decipher the intricate details of how the universe worked?

"After a certain high level of technical skill is achieved, science and art tend to coalesce in esthetics, plasticity, and form. The greatest scientists are always artists as well." – Albert Einstein (1879-1955)

Is that who prophets were? A people able to tap into a universe and see truths others could not and connect to another level of consciousness? A higher realm. We call such people prophets, visionaries and gifted. Every religion has such seers that lay the foundation of the religion – Buddha, Krishna, Jesus, Moses, Mohammed.

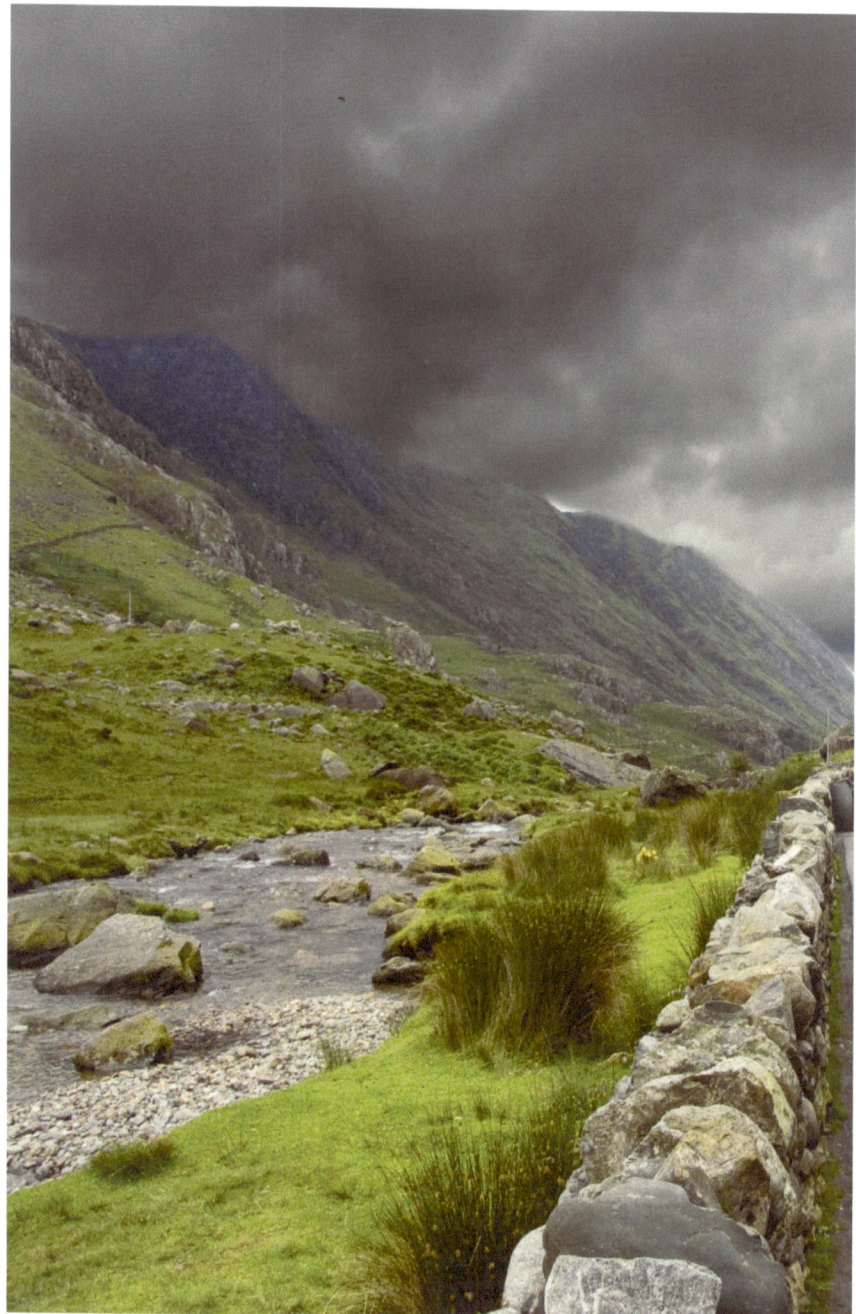

If such men could hypothetically congregate for a discussion – would they kill each other for their differences of practice? Or would they with a twinkle in their eye know that the most important thing in this world that each preached for successful living is "goodness". The rest were details of convenience for a time and a place which became religion.

Goodness is not always found where we would expect it. It is not always in the temples, mosques, synagogues, or churches – nor is it among academia in quantities one would expect. Being intelligent and gifted does not necessarily induce goodness. Most Scientists are very ordinary people once taken out of their area of specialization.

It is also not enough to be the brightest and the best. The only thing that matters that can move humanity forward is goodness. Who will argue that Hitler had great leadership skills – albeit we see the holocaust that can happen when it is not encompassed in goodness.

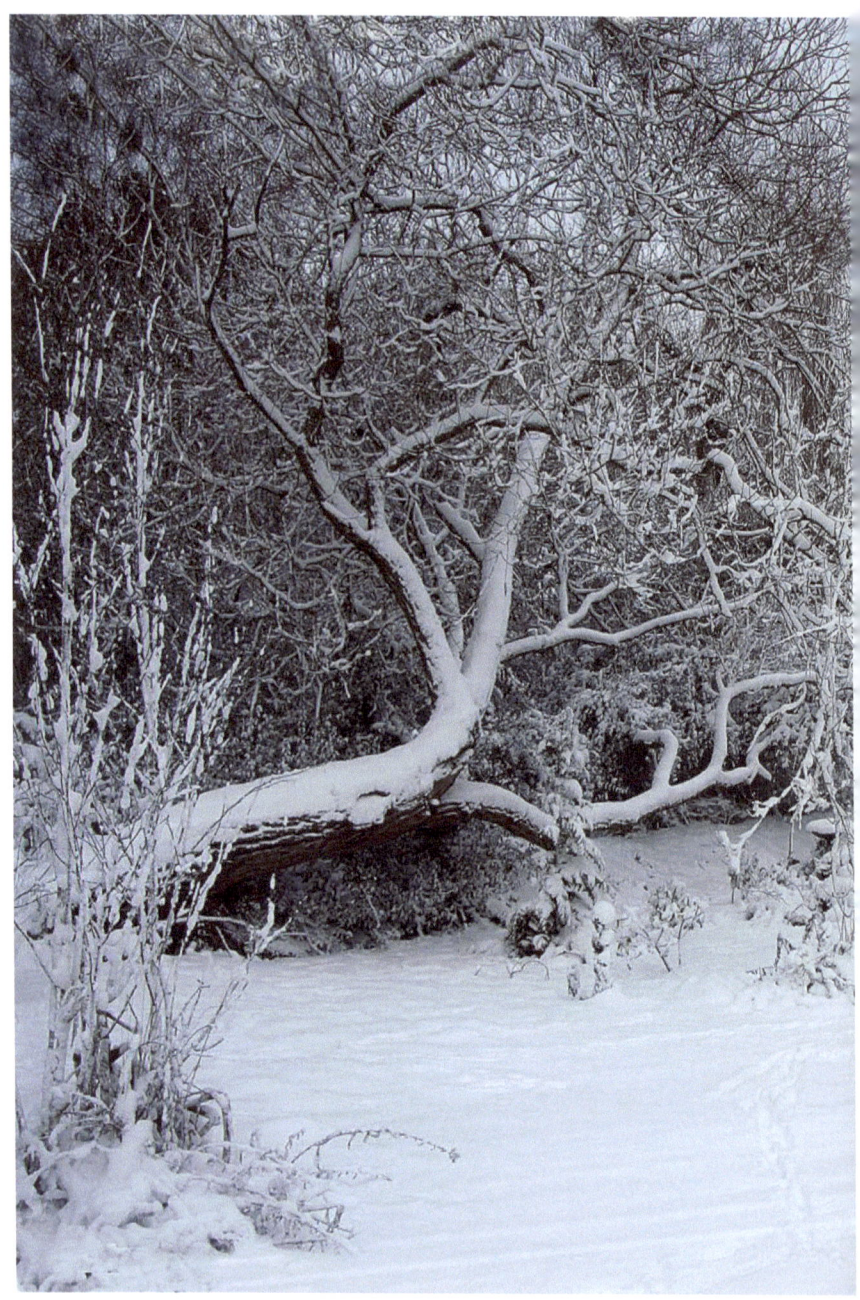

Does being endowed with gifts in this life know selection and bias? Evidence shows that gifted and good people come from anywhere, any gender, any race, and any religion. Gandhi, Martin Luther King, Joan of Arc, Nelson Mandela, Mother Theresa were all great and gifted people – a cut above the rest.

Any race, any religion, any gender. Oftentimes such people are killed by the very people whose condition they tried to lift – like Gandhi, Martin Luther King, Jesus, and John F. Kennedy.

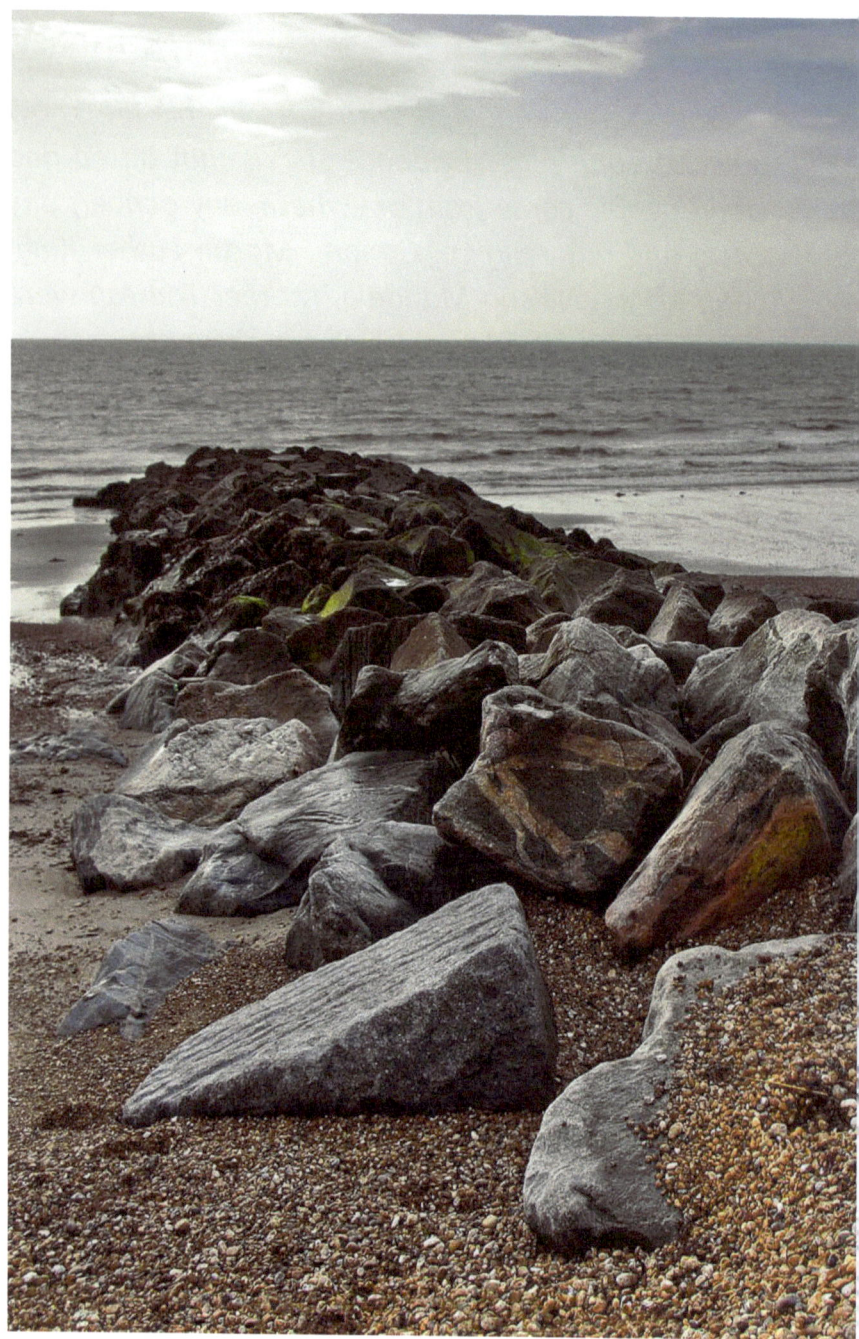

The evil thinkers

The scientists, people of knowledge, are notorious for being atheists yet the same "God" that grants them this gift does not take it from them for their disbelief.

How many gifted artists and singers are of sexual orientations frowned upon by religion?

The gifts are not taken from them and many leave the world a better and richer place than they found it or with a deeper understanding and imparted knowledge.

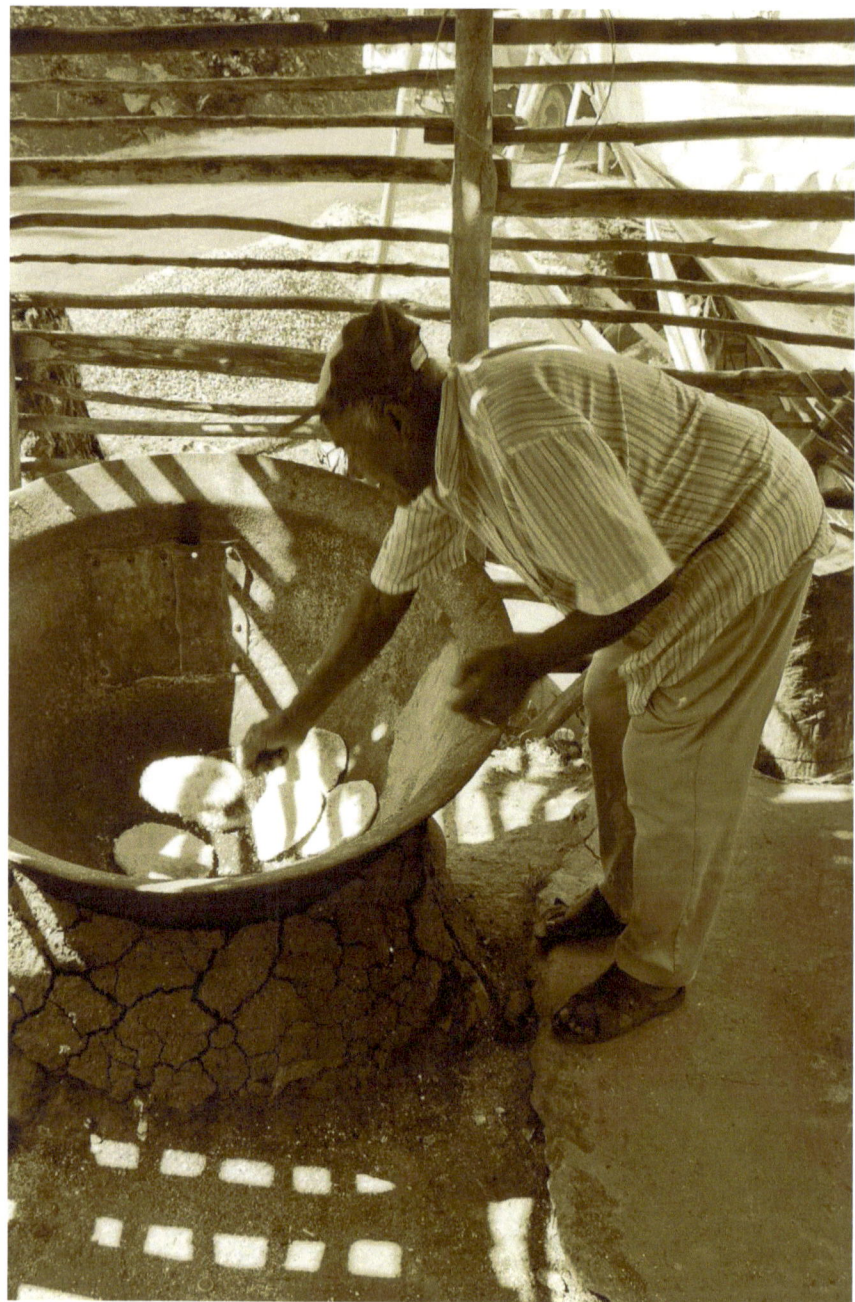

The evil doers

Why is it that in the most religious and sanctimonious places, we see sexual abuse of minors by men of God? Why could not the influence of religion in their lives have curtailed such perversion?

Is this evidence that genetic predisposition is a more powerful force than our belief and educational systems? Highly intelligent and educated people drink, smoke, gamble and practice sexual indiscretions despite the common knowledge of their detrimental effects. What drives such behavior ?

Clearly it is not enough to know what is the right thing to do.

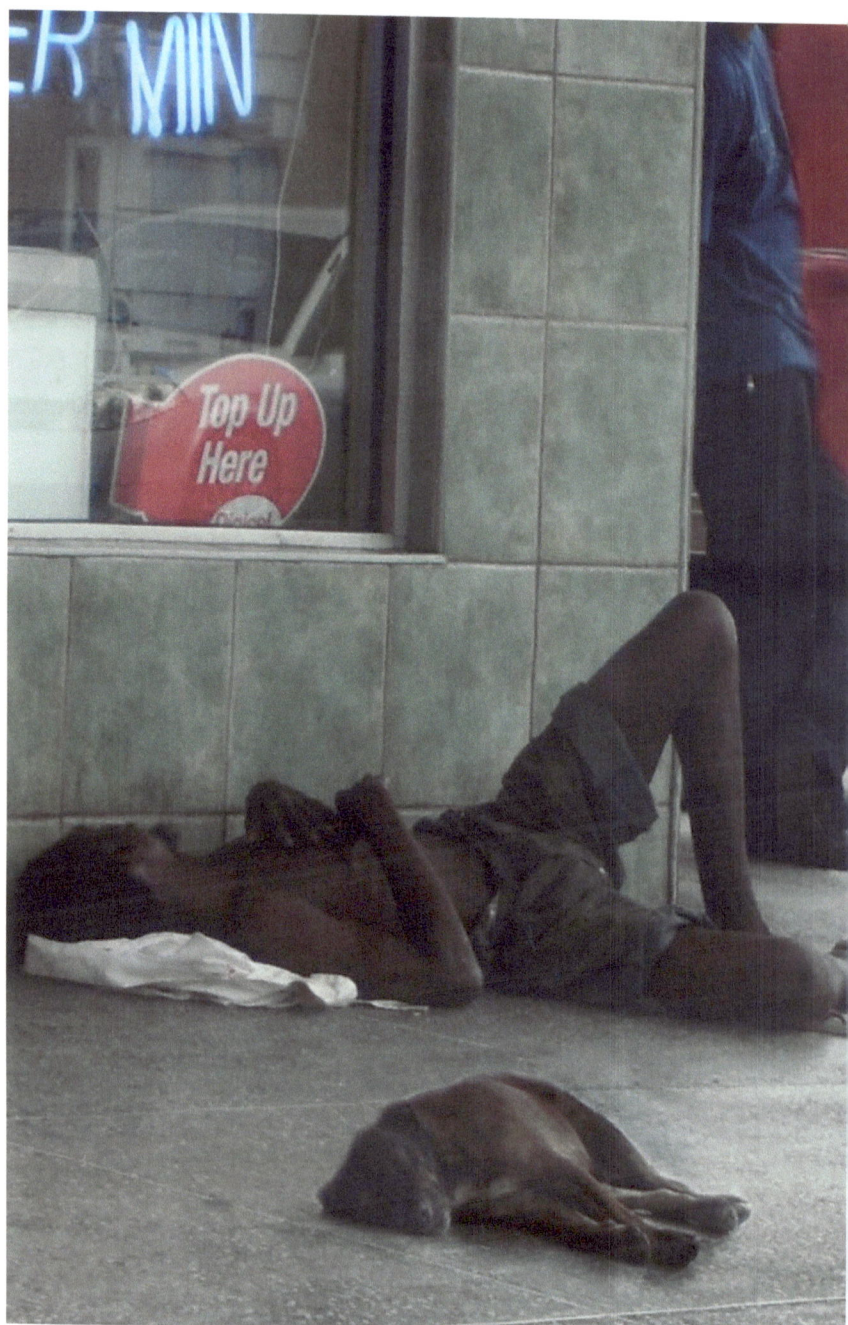

Baring our souls

Goodness knows no race, religion, gender, socio economic or educational status division. It is found in any place and among anyone. It is found in the person, who shares the little he has recognizing that someone else has less than him. That is goodness.

I have been given a first-hand account of when India was going through the partition into India and Pakistan, and Hindus were burning villages with Muslims in India. It was the neighboring village Hindus that hid their Muslim friends in their own homes to protect them from the pillage of their own people. Tears stream down the face of this elderly woman as she recounts this first hand. The Hindus that protected the Muslims were good to them.

Goodness is not in the clothes we wear, or the greetings we give or the places of worship we attend. What meaning is there to "spreading the word" in every religion, when the deeper intent is to perpetuate your dogma and arrogance of imagined superiority?

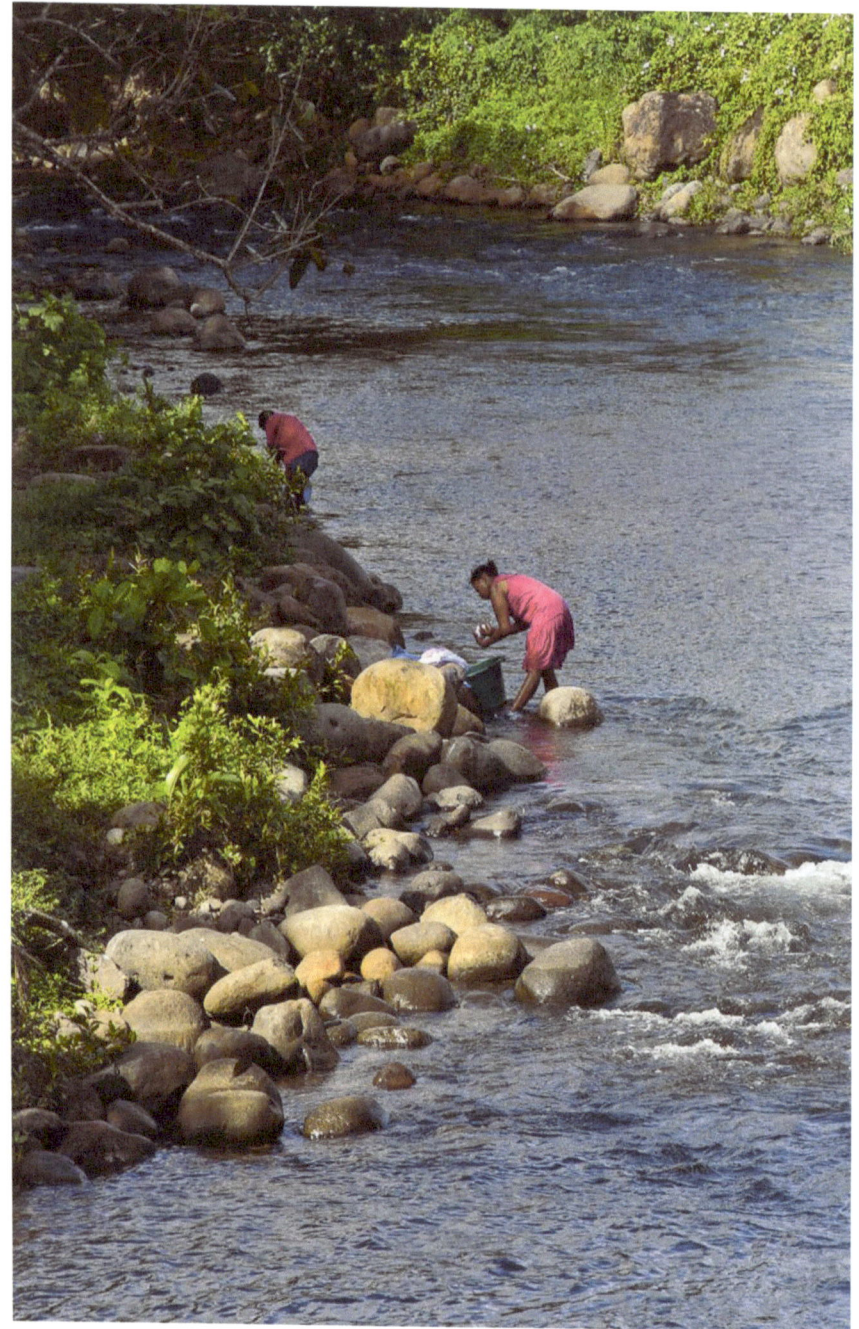

Imagine

The words of the song "Imagine" by John Lennon are deceptively simple yet deeply profound. He was gifted and a seer.

IMAGINE – John Lennon

*"Imagine there's no countries
It isn't hard to do
Nothing to kill or die for
And no religion too
Imagine all the people
Living life in peace..."*

Countries and religion – the two main reasons for waging war and killing countless of innocent people throughout the history of time.

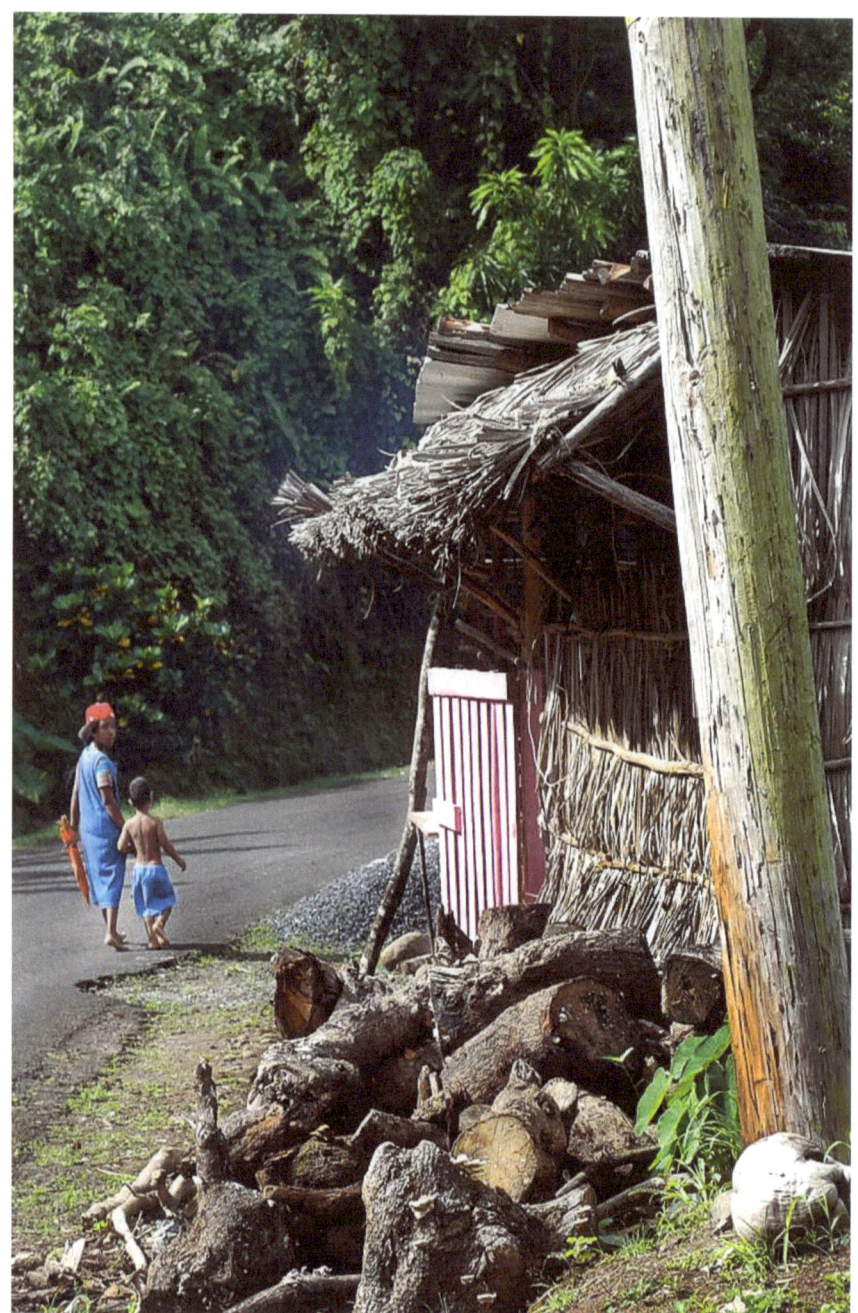

The greatest men and women among us are gifted and visionaries. They rise above lower order survival instincts of jealousy, territory, envy, pride and arrogance – all aspects that have their role in personal survival, yet, act as detriments to the growth of a system or unit, or country.

For how can a system move forward if every element composing that system is concerned about itself alone and pulling in discordant directions rather than pulling together. It must become "what about you?" over "what about me?" if "we" are to move forward.

If each of us could give more than we take, what strides we would make!

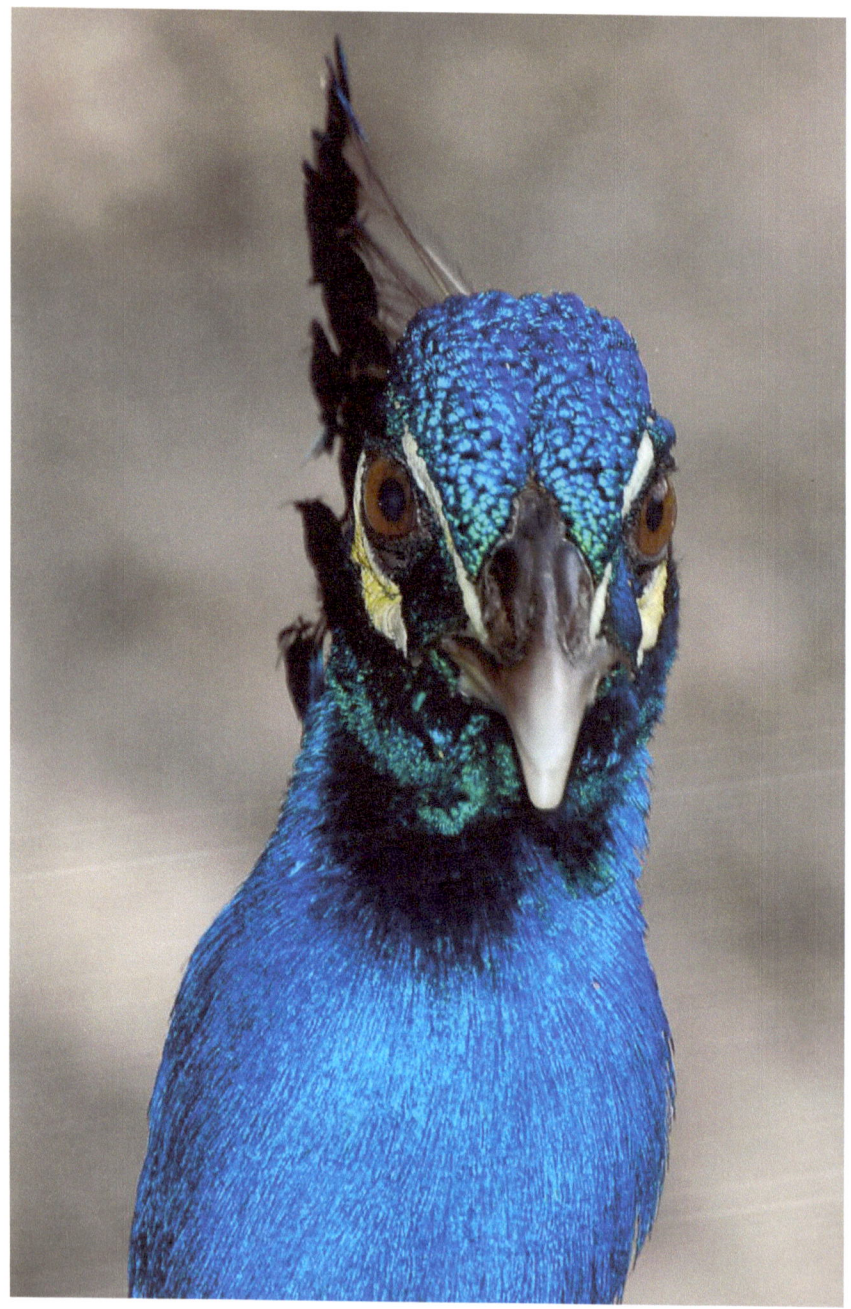

Walking among mortals

Why is sex, power and money such motivating factors for much of the behavior of most humans? Are these the primal genetic coding that religion seeks to suppress? Power, control and domination. Few things can destroy and eat away at any system like those when they become part of the dynamics. It mitigates against trust and goodwill. The driving force for goodness to propagate.

Our sense of self – is a very powerful thing that directs how we behave and the strength of our belief. Barring the minority of persons with low self-esteem, most persons sense of self is so powerful that it is unshakeable and like the opening lines from the book 'When Prophecy Fails' by Leon Festinger,

"A man with a conviction is a hard man to change. Tell him you disagree and he turns away. Show him facts or figures and he questions your sources. Appeal to logic and he fails to see your point."

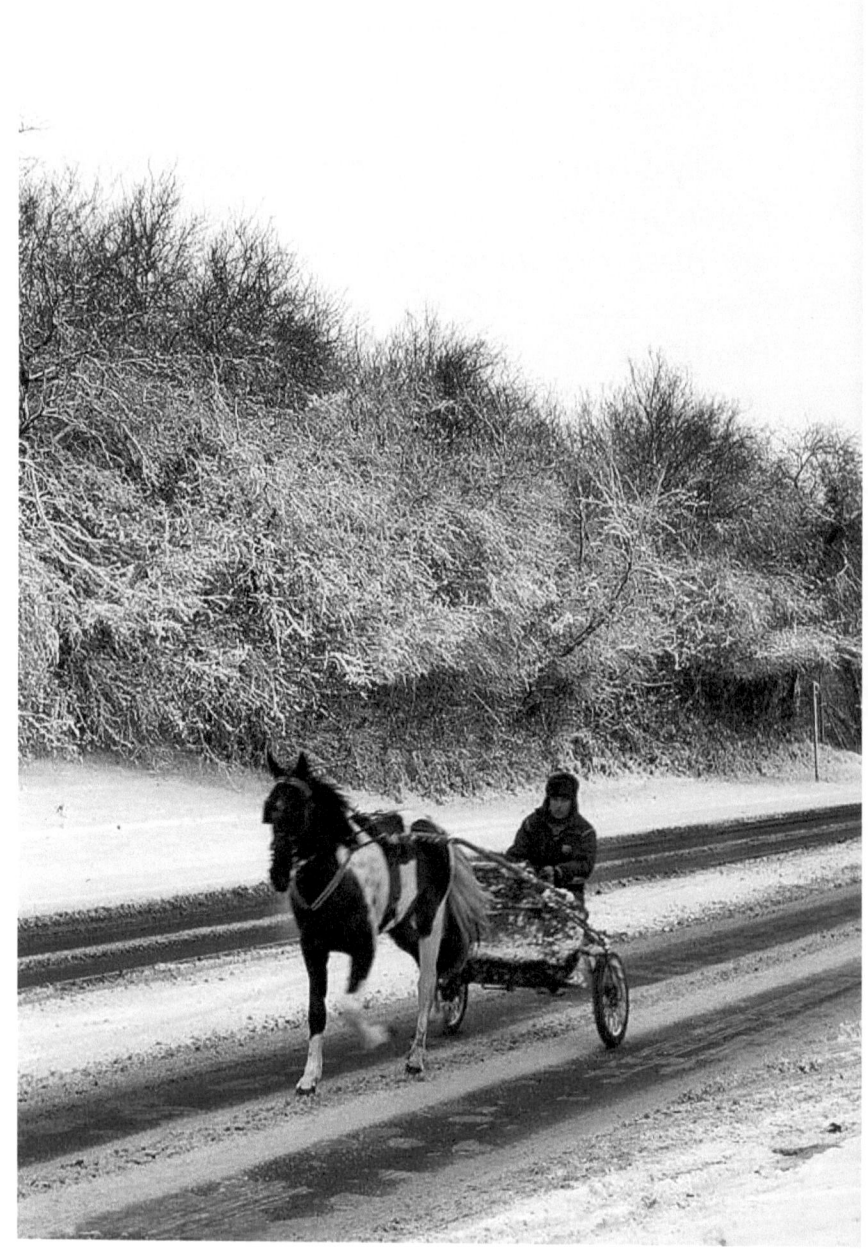

So we fight, we complain about the behavior of others and defend ourselves furiously to justify our positions and actions...and like-minded people gather together and become friends to reinforce each other and their belief system which sometimes appear as utter madness to another group.

In an extreme form, this becomes the cult —but religion often hovers dangerously close to the boundaries of such if left unchecked. Loyalty is about not questioning the status quo.

Such loyalty and belief in the wisdom of others caused humanity to believe for thousands of years that the sun went around the earth - what courage, what spirit it takes for the lone academic entrepreneur to even consider an alternative – and here too is the power of logic, rationale and thought.

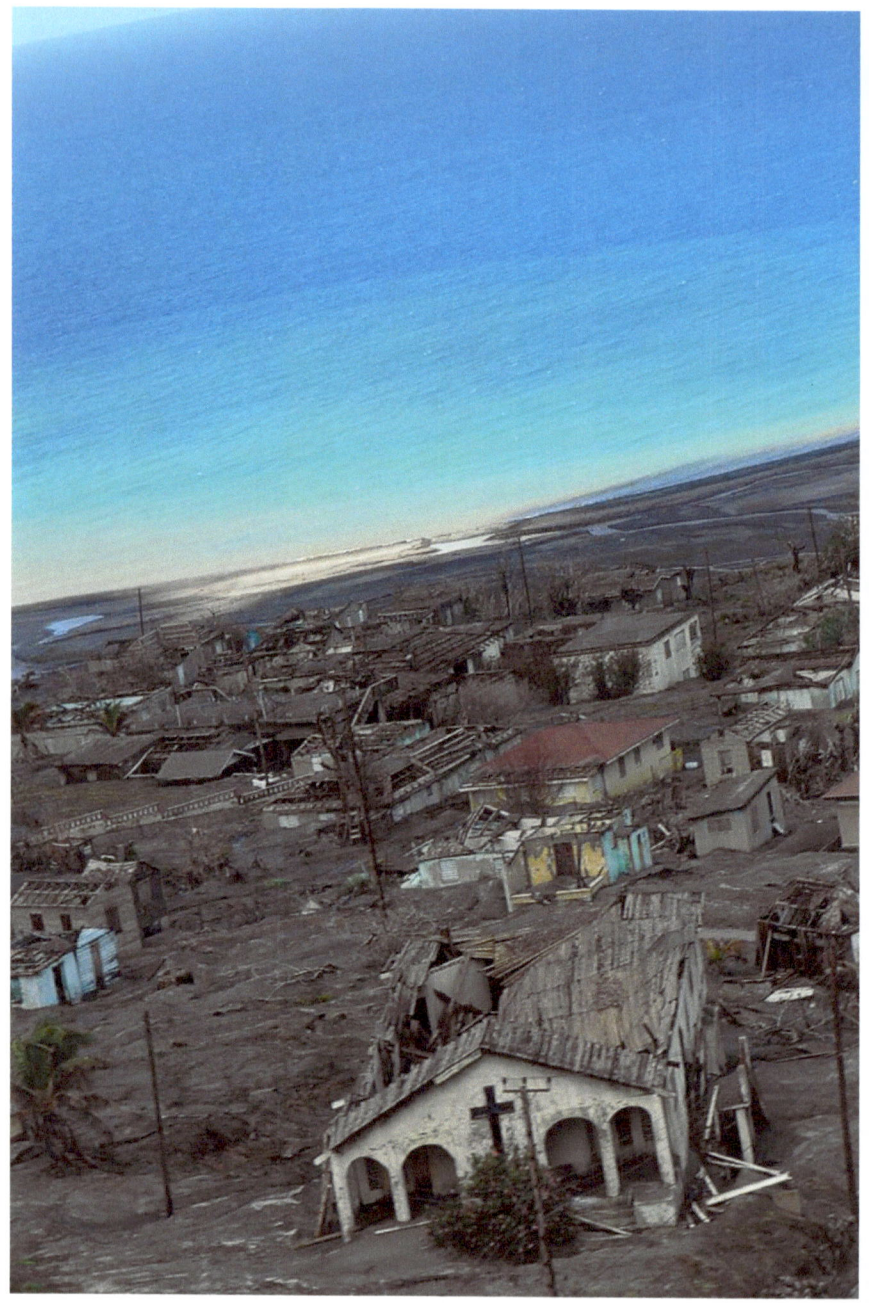

Depths of our souls

Group-think mitigates against diversity – yet genetics' most powerful weapon has been to mutate and diversify and adapt.

Yet, whether it is in politics or religion, the brainwash of group-think is propagated and it is done most subtly through the most powerful means of all – the emotions.

If at our fundamental levels and at the heart of our biological selves we are all similar- that whether you are black, white or brown, male or female your biology is the same, why then would that same god who created that, subscribe a difference in treatment of each and subordination of one over another?

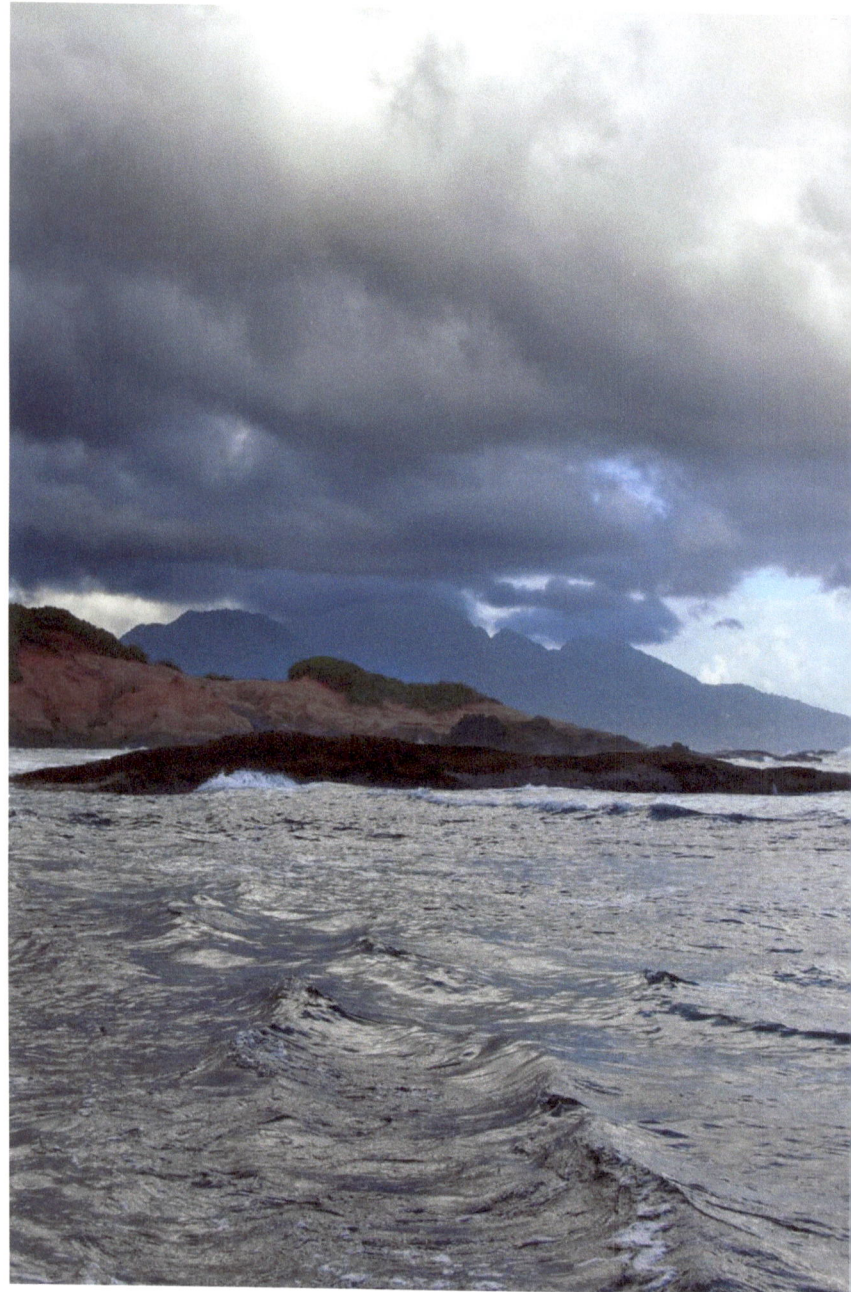

The single hardest thing to understand is how humans can inflict untold pain and punishment upon their own. If a person has erred or sinned, why do not the religious people leave the punishment up to the lord once the transgressor is not a risk or harm to others? After all, the most cruel punishments come from the religious themselves – burning witches at stake, hangings, stoning to death, and beheading. How many have suffered for their ideas and loyalties and consensual sexual transgression between adults, that was not someone else's idea of right? If one hurts none but themselves, why should we take the onus of bringing justice to them?

Let the god that set the rules, arbitrate if you truly believe in the hereafter and judgment and the afterlife and in Him. To punish in this life is to not believe that God will yield that justice or the rightful justice. The religious have imbued more power unto themselves than even their own God. They have become God and wield justice!

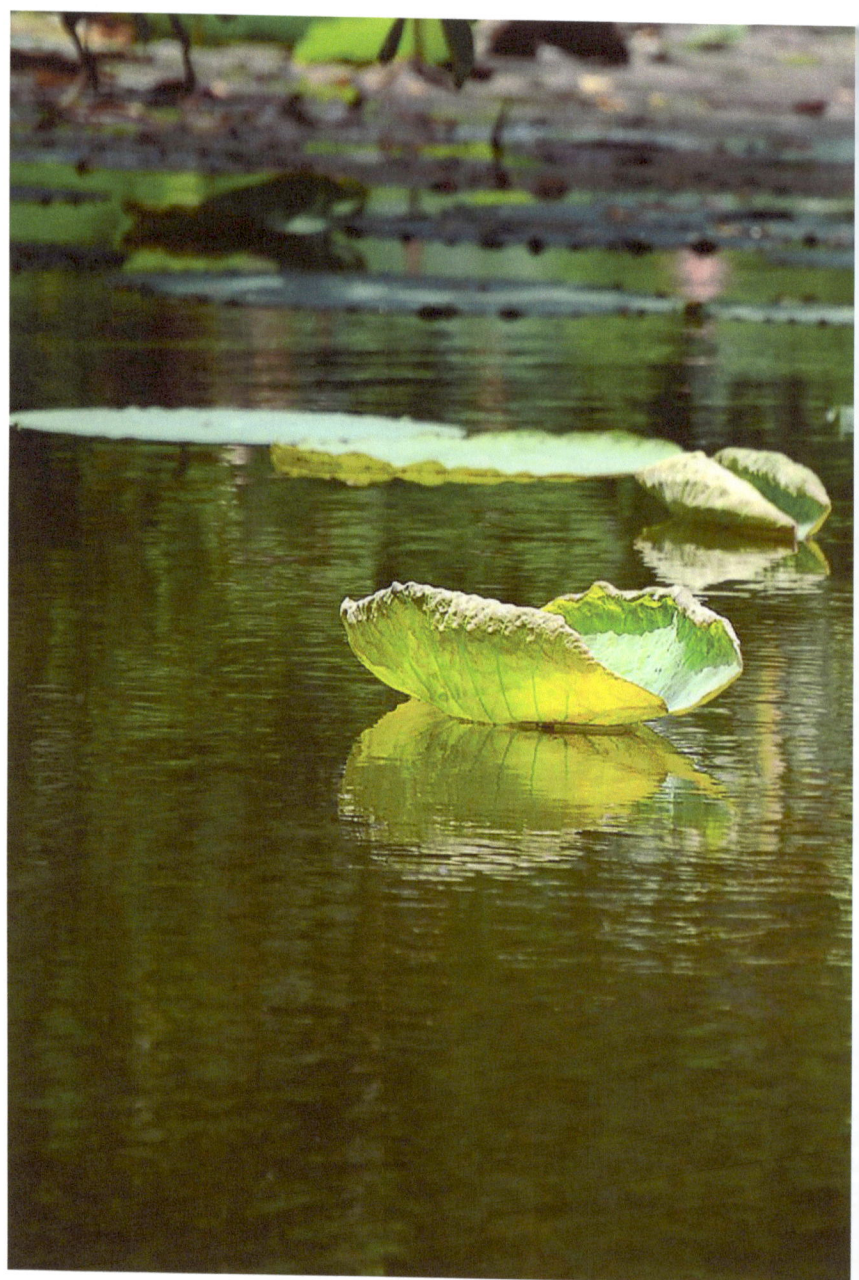

How do you treat the church-going believing person that does wrong and hurts others? How do you treat the disbeliever that helps those in need?

The burning question becomes, on which end of the scale tips – has religion hurt or helped our progression as a human race?

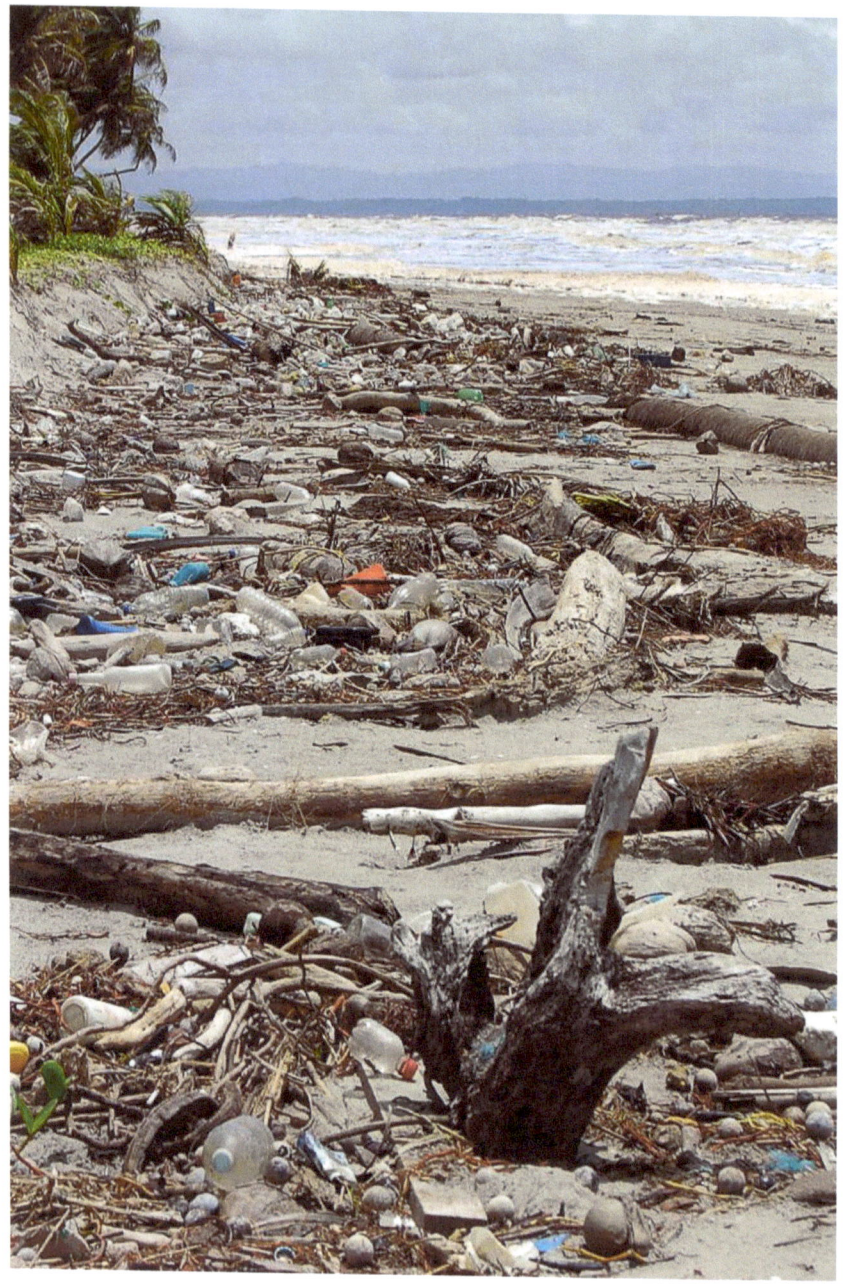

Eupsychia

Truth, Goodness and Beauty – the epitome of life. Two of the three being hallmarks of good science – truth and beauty. Enveloped in goodness, humanity can make progress armed with the knowledge of truth through science as never before for better living for all inhabitants of planet Earth during our visit here. If we would only allow ourselves, and stop being occupied with "My religion, and my way is better than yours".

Where does this fountain of goodness towards humanity come from? It comes from a deep sense of cosmic religiousness and a sense of responsibility which knows that to serve humanity is a higher calling than to be served. To pause at the wonder of creation in awe is a prayer in its own right. Goodness has its seeds in a thing called "selfless love" and "conscience". A gift known amazingly only by the human species – as long as we do not sabotage our own existence and destroy ourselves into oblivion. Science, Religion and Life are really in the final analysis, nothing more than Truth, Goodness and Beauty in practice respectively.

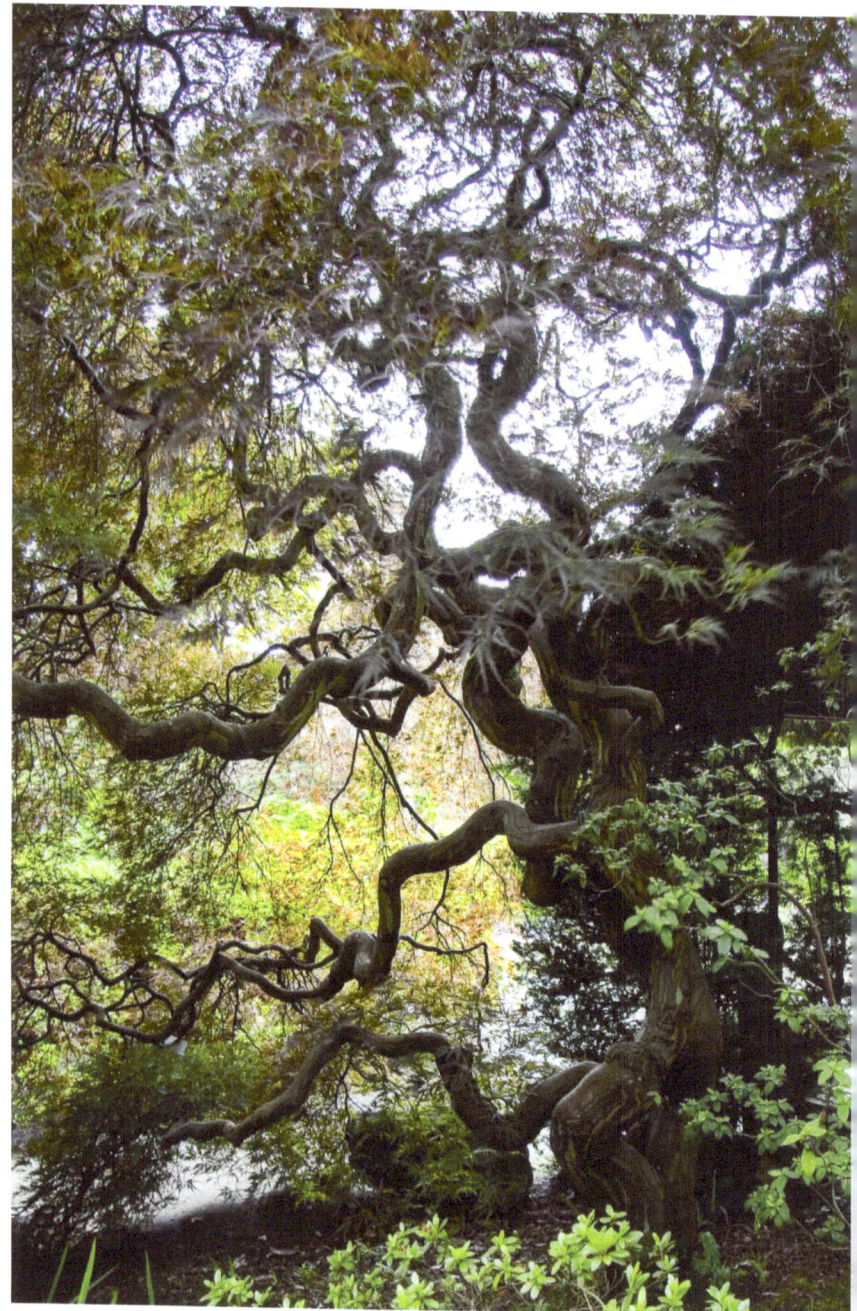

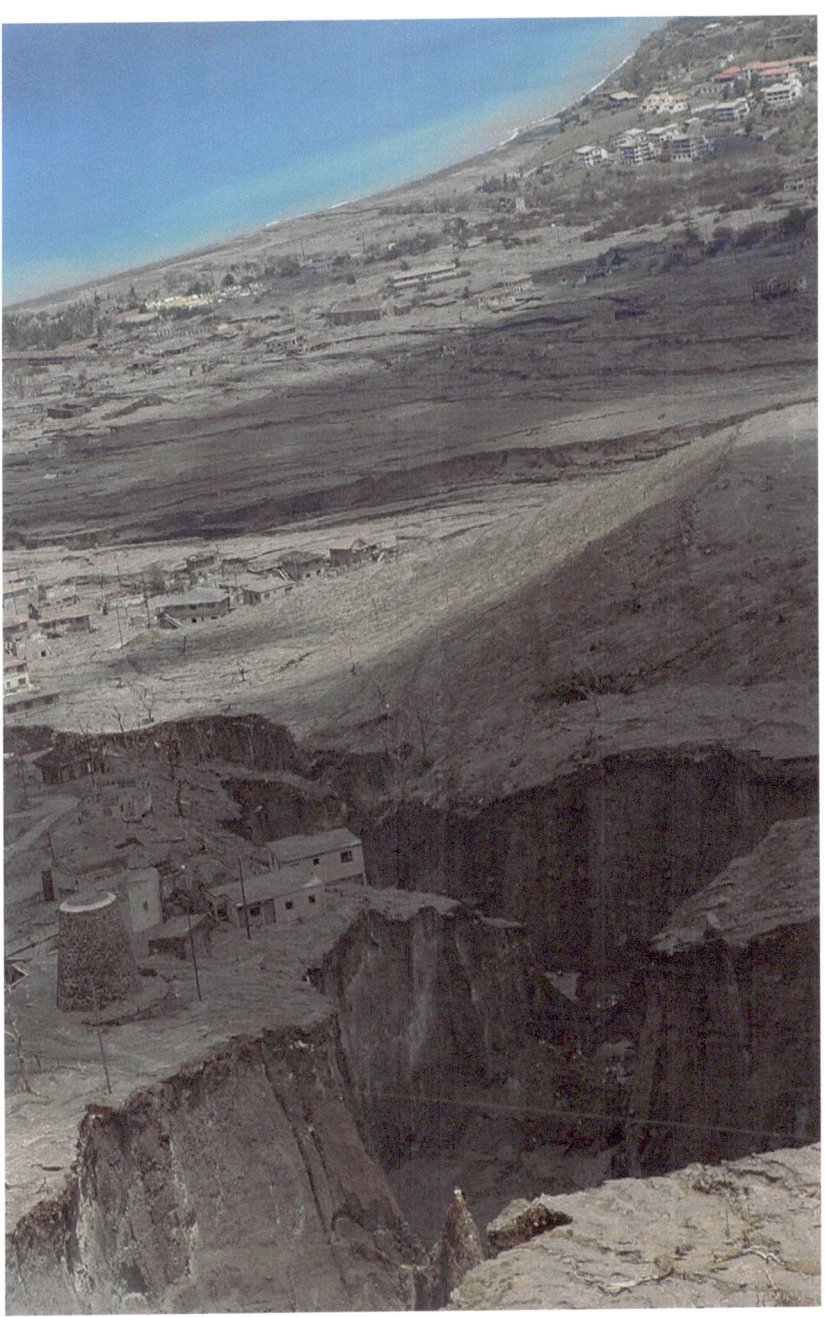